P9-DUK-640

AMERICA'S SCHOOLS
AND THE MASS MEDIA

AMERICA'S SCHOOLS AND THE MASS MEDIA

Edited by

Everette E. Dennis
Craig L. LaMay

Transaction Publishers
New Brunswick (U.S.A.) and London (U.K.)

Copyright © 1993 by Transaction Publishers, New Brunswick, New Jersey 08903. Originally published in the *Gannett Center Journal*, Winter 1991, Copyright © 1991 by The Freedom Forum Media Studies Center and The Freedom Forum.

All rights reserved under International and Pan-American Copyright Conventions. No part of this book may be reproduced or transmitted in any form or by any means, electronic or mechanical, including photocopy, recording, or any information storage and retrieval system, without prior permission in writing from the publisher. All inquiries should be addressed to Transaction Publishers, Rutgers—The State University, New Brunswick, New Jersey 08903.

Library of Congress Catalog Number: 92-28070
ISBN: 1-56000-652-8
Printed in the United States of America

Library of Congress Cataloging-in-Publication Data
America's schools and the mass media / edited by Everette E. Dennis, Craig L. LaMay.
    p. c.m.
   ISBN: 1-56000-652-8 (paper)
    1. Education in mass media—United States.   2. Mass media in education—United States.   I. Dennis, Everette E.   II. LaMay, Craig L.
P96.E292U63   1992
370'973—dc20
                                     92-28070
                                          CIP

Contents

Simply put, "the more important an educational question is, the less people know about it," argues the author, an education scholar with long experience in school-labor disputes. Anyone concerned with the state of the nation's schools — or the school down the block — "can safely ignore most of the education issues that currently receive media attention."

Part I Education in the Media

Newspaper editors typically rate the education beat as one of the most important, but in fact education stories rarely receive prominent play and reporters and editors alike treat the beat as a professional purgatory. A communications researcher examines the findings from a study of the top editors at nearly 300 U.S. dailies.

"To our op-ed page analysts, educational reform customarily means dragging the schools back a half-century as rapidly as possible," says the author, a Washington-based education writer. "If old-fashioned, no-non-sense schools worked for them, why shouldn't they succeed for today's children?"

In a gubernatorial race that drew national attention, Illinois Republican Jim Edgar made education a cornerstone of his campaign. But the state's news media mostly ignored his reform proposals and focused instead on an education tax surcharge. "In a nation where the education of our young people will be one of the most important concerns of the next decade,"

Edgar asks, "will the media be willing to examine all the problems affecting education in depth, especially within the context of campaigns for major public office?"

"It's a curious paradox that educators regard television, simultaneously, with awe and contempt," writes a former education correspondent, now with The Learning Channel. "Widely acknowledged as the most powerful educational tool ever invented, television has almost from the beginning been derided as a 'wasteland' and worse." But blaming television for the failure of our schools is not only wrong, it ignores the medium's value as a pedagogic tool.

Crossword puzzles on collective bargaining from the Teamsters? Instructional videos from the United Farm Workers? Such products are only two of thousands of "educational" materials developed by corporations, governments and interest groups for use in elementary and high school classrooms. A public relations researcher looks at the long and questionable history of information campaigns in public schools.

"Through a funhouse mirror, '80s movies set in high school reflected disturbing social realities — about the power of commercial youth culture, about authority, about the powerful dividers of class and race. And they could make you feel downright sorry for the teacher." A communications scholar looks at the "kidpix" version of America's schools.

In an era of budget shortfalls and declining student enrollments, interactive television instruction may prove to be more than another whiz-bang technology, say the authors, a communications scholar and school superintendent. "ITV is a transformation of the instructional environment that offers new opportunities to extend the coverage of talented teachers, to gain economies of scale by sharing resources among schools, and economies of scope by extending the curricula of schools, especially small or rural ones."

Part II Education into the 21st Century

Six leading figures in the worlds of education and media answer a question simple to ask but infinitely more difficult to answer: "What are the most important educational issues of the 1990s?"

"With major U.S. corporations now competing on a global basis," argues *Time* magazine's education writer, "it seems dangerously out-of-date to maintain one set of standards for students in one state and a different set in another. As newspaper and magazine readers found out after digesting a spate of stories about the 1983 federal report *A Nation at Risk*, it is indeed the country that is in trouble, not Michigan or Oklahoma."

The images that the media captured in the years following *Brown vs. Board of Education*, at Little Rock, Ole Miss and elsewhere, are indelibly etched into the national memory. But the agenda facing civil rights and educational activists in the 1990s has so far failed to produce reporting of comparable intensity or engagement. A veteran civil rights reporter looks at how the issues have changed in the 37 years since *Brown*, noting that today some black leaders who seek quality education for their children believe that separate schooling may be the better way to achieve it.

"Every major business group in the country is talking about education, and virtually every major corporation in America is actively involved in trying to make improvements," writes the author, an education reporter and former deputy business editor for the *Detroit Free Press*. Businesses are putting millions of dollars into everything from buildings and computers to employment and mentor programs. But to whom are they accountable and what are their goals? Who's watching and what's going on?

"School choice" has been a part of educational reform rhetoric in one form or another for at least 30 years, though the idea of using public funds to pay for education at private schools supposedly died out with the Reagan administration. Now the idea is back, says an official with the American Federation of Teachers — the result of a single book, a public relations venture, and a predictable swell of uncritical and unsophisticated news coverage.

Part III

Education reporting has been criticized for decades for its failure to describe what goes on in the classroom and how children learn. Here an education scholar and former *Washington Post* reporter examines the world of teachers and students through the work of three journalists, a gifted teacher and a social scientist. "The collective portrait that emerges," says the author, "tells us more about the real stuff of teaching and learning than can be found in a roomful of reform reports."

Preface

Any quotation dictionary that includes an "education" entry provides ample testimony that education is more than schools. From Aristotle to Wilde come warnings that education is no substitute for experience, even that formal education is antithetical to learning. George Bernard Shaw says it succinctly in his quip that "the only time my education was interrupted was when I was in school."

Journalists who cover education might find such sarcasm reassuring, since in their reporting on primary and secondary schools they are likely to write considerably more on administrative, financial, legal or social issues than about learning. The public learns about school boards, teacher strikes, fiscal crises, standardized test scores, drugs and violence, but there is little empathetic coverage of young people engaged in the learning process.

Of course it is almost axiomatic today that stories about "process" are beyond the media's ability to do well. The criticism that education news is woefully substandard in this regard has been around for at least 40 years; education stories are often retrospective, a working backward from product or problem — from the news itself. The Soviet Union's 1957 success with the unmanned earth-orbiter Sputnik, for instance, became a focal point for an earlier drive to improve America's schools; but then as now the nation's goals were shaped around an agenda that had less to do with education than with economic competition and national security. Today, American high school students are by most qualitative or quantitative measures poorly suited to life in a competitive marketplace. Consequently much of the national debate on education, and media coverage of the same, focuses on the management of the "factory," the training and retention of its labor force, and the distribution of its resources. One need only point to rhetorical roar over "restructuring," the current buzzword of the public schooling business.

Another factor influencing education coverage is the knowledge that comes from our personal experience, both as students and as parents. Most citizens will quickly tell you that they think education is important and that it ought to have high priority in public policy; however it is also true that most people think their own schools are fine — it's the school in the next town that has problems. A similar kind of cognitive dissonance exists in news coverage. When asked, most editors rank education among their most important beats; but at the same time, as a survey reported here indicates, the beat has little status and is typically covered by young, inexperienced reporters. The beat is simply not the pathway to leadership in news organizations that, say, the political beat is.

Of course there is more to the relationship between America's schools and the mass media than news coverage. At another level our whole communications system, its "hardware" and "software," are instruments of education. Newspapers, broadcast and cable television both inform and teach, and all have been employed with mixed motives and varying success as classroom tools. "Newspaper in the Classroom" programs help foster interest in public affairs at the same time that they inculcate the newspaper habit in a new generation of readers. Chris Whittle's controversial "Channel One" television venture has underscored the poverty of the debate over public school purpose, in the process obscuring some of the more positive developments in television's development as an educational, even a pedagogically valuable, medium.

The Channel One controversy has also underscored the political nature of American public education, which, as a topic of national policy, is almost never seriously discussed as an issue of learning. Rather it is the rubric under which a range of other issues play themselves out or are niched into the curriculum — in the form of drivers' education or AIDS prevention classes, for example — and it is more than ever a proving ground for the aspirations of private interests and corporations.

However political this cacophonous debate may be, it is nonetheless an important one; it will determine who controls our schools. It leaves unresolved and often unaddressed, however, the ages-old question of what constitutes a good education or what its purpose should be.

American public schooling, finally, has historical roots as a crucible for democratic government, an ideal that has not only grown increasingly suspect in recent years, but which is now commonly assailed as a brake on both economic growth and intellectual excellence. If Jefferson's vision of universal education has become an expensive folly, we must ask ourselves what minimum skills and knowledge one need possess in order to participate in the life of the nation, if not in the life of the mind. For the most part journalists have yet to think seriously about these questions, a shortcoming that greatly hinders intelligent coverage of education's processes and the people who shape them.

This volume begins with an assertion: "The more important an educational question is, the less people know about it." So says "Lieberman's Law," the unhappy but unshakable conclusion of more than 40 years' experience in the life of an education scholar and school labor negotiator, Myron Lieberman.

The following section, "Education in the Media," illustrates Lieberman's lament, examining some of the paradoxes and prejudices created by the interplay of educational and media institutions. In "The Twilight Zone Beat," NBC audience researcher Lawrence McGill surveys editors at 300 U.S. daily newspapers and finds the education beat to be a kind of professional purgatory. Education also gets rhetorical rumbles from the nation's leading pundits, writes George Kaplan in "Oh, When I Was Young!" and it fares no better as a matter of official concern, as Illinois Governor Jim Edgar points out in "Reading, Writing and Taxes," his reflection on the education debate that was central to his 1990 gubernatorial campaign.

Other media/education issues go beyond the schools, as Shaw might say, and concern what students learn and how they learn it. In "Title Goes Here," the Learning Channel's John Merrow asks teachers to think again about the pedagogical power of television; and public relations scholar Charles Salmon looks at the long and questionable history of corporate, special interest and government attempts to shape the beliefs of future citizens and consumers through school-based information campaigns. Salmon's vision of value-warfare finds cinematic expression in Patricia Aufderheide's essay "Hollywood High," which examines the "kidpix" world of commercial youth culture, authority, class and race. Finally, Fred and Victoria Williams, a communications scholar and a school superintendent, respectively, look at the social, administrative and curricular benefits of interactive television instruction (ITV) in their essay "Amo, Amas . . . Amazing!"

The final section, "Education into the 21st Century," opens with an informal survey: Six leading figures in the worlds of education and media offer their views on the nation's educational priorities. Following them, three journalists and a social scientist write in more detail on issues they believe require better media coverage: *Time*'s Susan Tifft aruges for national school standards; civil rights reporter Michele Magar looks at the idea of of seperate schooling for black males; Joan Richardson of the *Detroit Free Press* writes on the push of Corporate America to transform the nation's educational system; and Bella Rosenberg of the American Federation of Teachers critiques the free-market twist of an old idea, "school choice."

Lastly, this volume includes a book review which considers the long-standing criticism that education reporting fails to describe what goes on in the classroom. In "Brain Checking," education scholar and former *Washington Post* reporter Gerald Grant reviews the world of teachers and students through the work of three journalists, a teacher and a social scientist. "While such a sample may not be scientific," Grant writes, "the collective portrait that emerges tells us more about the real stuff of teaching and learning than can be found in a roomful of reform reports. The struggles these teachers waged to educate some of the poorest children in the United States also reveal deep truths about what ails us."

THE EDITORS

Introduction:
Media and America's Schools

Media and this nation's schools can be seen as allies in the same army, both concerned with literacy and the promulagation of information. On the other hand, they can also be seen as wary competitors, in a mutual struggle to get the upper hand in shaping the public's thinking and behavior.

For the media, schools K through 12 are a topic of news and entertainment. Most newspapers have an education editor and purport to cover the schools, paying attention to how they are financed and administered and how well they are doing their job. In most communities, such coverage is routine and uncontroversial. But on occasion, schools are the subject of intense controversy — crime and drugs in the schools, strikes by teacher's unions, protests by parents. In many communities, schools are also the number one priority and largest expenditure of local government, and therefore the subject of continuous scrutiny.

Yet there are flaws in education coverage. A few years ago, a study of U.S. newspaper editors asked them what the most important story was in their community. The most common answer was "education," or "the schools." Sadly, however, the same study reported that even in the face of these views, the same editors devoted little attention or resources to covering school and educational issues.

When the media look at schools, they see news stories and story lines for television dramas and sitcoms. From television's beginning, schools have often been depicted in television fare. From "Our Miss Brooks" to "Welcome Back, Kotter", Hollywood scriptwriters have found schools an irresistible source of material. After all, they are filled with attractive young people in the prime of life. They are also the setting for social problems — from family dislocation to violence of all kinds.

The opinion media, which includes newspaper editorial pages, magazines, and talk radio, are also interested in schools and frequently say so. Editorialists express strong views of what schools ought to do, and to what extent they need or deserve public support. Radio talk show hosts report what happens in the schools and debate it long into the night. This is natural because schools bring people together; that is, all children must at some time go to school, and everyone has at some time been a student.

From the perspective of the schools and the people therein, the media are an important means of communication. Schools, as represented by administrators, teachers and parents, want to be portrayed accurately (and usually that means favorably) in the press. They want the news media to convey to the public a representative picture of what schools do, and how well they do it. They want support for their budget, physical plants, and teachers' salaries. But often, spokespersons for schools end up complaining that they are not treated fairly or responsibly. They say schools only make news when something bizarre or untoward happens, and that superficial apsects of school life are given priority over deep and pervasive problems.

Educators who watch the coverage of schools with an attentive eye complain that not only do education reporters lack experience with the subject they are covering, but that they also engage in a game of musical chairs. As one principal said, "just when I get a young reporter broken in, fully initiated to what is happening in the schools, they move onto another beat and I have to start again." Indeed, for only a few reporters nationwide is education a satisfying permanent beat. It is either a stepping stone to larger assignments or a dead end for reporters not up to what are deemed more important assignments.

So we are left with two of society's principal institutions eyeing each other with fascination, but also with a disturbing level of superficiality and even distrust. Fortunately, there are exceptions. A few years ago, the editors of *Newsday*, a distinguished newspaper on Long Island, New York, decided that covering schools in a fragmented fashion had little utility. Thus, they began thinking not about covering schools and school boards, of which there were many in their circulation area, but about treating education in a holistic fashion, covering it across two counties in terms of issues, problems, and controversies. In this way, there was less emphasis on the singular instances of a given school board its problems. Attention was instead given to students and their needs, teachers and the way they do their work, the choice of curricula, sports and other extracurricular activities, as well as the two overarching topics, governance and financing, that were always the stuff of news coverage.

It is in the spirit of that kind of innovative journalistic venture that we in this volume look at media and America's schools, as they look warily at each other.

1

Lieberman's Law

Myron Lieberman

Somewhere in the third decade of my professional experience with education I formulated Lieberman's Law: The more important an educational question is, the less people know about it. I wasn't happy with the Law, and I've spent 20 years thinking about it. It still stands.

At a rhetorical level, everyone agrees that good information is essential to good education ("good information" being not only straightforward factual data but insightful analysis of facts and policies, actual and proposed). Moreover when the government provides education — of approximately 75,000 government jurisdictions in the United States about 15,000 are school boards — educational policies are public policies, hence all the caveats about the importance of an informed citizenry come into play. Inasmuch as mayors, governors, state and federal legislatures, presidents and a host of other public officials also play critical roles in education, education and politics are inextricably linked. Needless to say, media play an important role with respect to both candidates and issues.

It is important to note here that the "liberal"/"conservative" split is largely irrelevant to the problem of educational information in the mass media. Even if education were provided through a market system, as some supporters of education vouchers have envisioned, information issues would be paramount. For the past 30 years at least, public interest in private schools has grown, and although few if any analysts believe that private schools could completely replace public schools in the foreseeable future, political and educational debate frequently focuses on proposals to enlarge the role of private schools. Proposals to provide

5

parents with greater choice of the public schools their children attend are also receiving considerable attention at local, state and national levels of educational policy.

Whatever the merits of such proposals, the availability of reliable information about schools is a highly controversial issue in the debate over them. In this connection, one hardly need point out that reliable information is a *sine qua non* of market economics. In fact, the earliest and perhaps the most insightful criticism of socialist economic systems was that they would fail because their information systems do not rely on market prices to regulate supply and demand. As most economists see it, market prices are an information system. They tell us what consumers want and how much or how little they want it. Prices also reveal the costs of meeting various consumer preferences.

Public education has no price system, a fact that underscores the importance of media to the way it functions. Instead of prices in a market system, legislators, school boards, parents and taxpayers alike rely partly on the media to guide their actions. To be sure, this is an oversimplification, and information is not the sole determinant of educational policy; individual and group interests often support different actions and policies, even with the same information. Nevertheless I believe it fair to say that neglect of information issues is perhaps the single most important reason why the educational reform movement of the 1980s failed to achieve significant results.

If my perception of the importance of media is correct, the implication is paradoxical, to say the least. The individuals in media who control the flow of information and opinion about education are extremely important actors in the educational scene; in my opinion the most powerful and influential educational position in the United States is education editor of the *New York Times*. Nevertheless, neither the *Times* nor the other leading newspapers and newsmagazines that employ full-time education reporters and editors requires a background in educational policy or research or even in the culture of education as a prerequisite to employment in the position. Whether on-the-job training suffices is highly debatable; after all, who among other media personnel has the sophistication or the incentive to raise the issue? In fact the strongest disincentives exist to avoid it. Most education reporters and editors explicitly reject the view that any issue exists. I have even encountered education editors, responsible for what millions of Americans read on the subject, who assert that educational expertise would be a handicap. The reason for this astonishing conclusion is that such individuals would supposedly write for other educational specialists, not for a large lay audience.

At first cut, the question of media's relationship to education appears to be: What do the American people know about education and how well does their knowledge prepare them to fulfill their roles as sponsors, monitors and consumers of public education? This formulation, however, erroneously assumes that the basic information issues can be resolved or answered by a snapshot of citizen sophistication about education at any given time. As with other public policy issues, new circumstances, new problems, new technology and new research can emerge at any time. Consequently we must look at educational information from a systems perspective and consider such issues as:

- Who produces what kind of educational information?

- How is educational information transmitted, disseminated, stored and retrieved?

- Who pays for educational information and/or who supports the information system?

- Who uses educational information, and for what purposes?

- What educational information is produced — and what is not produced?

- How accurate and how useful is our educational information?

In referring to an "information system" I do not mean to suggest that all the actors are under unified control. They're not, any more than buyers and sellers are under unified control in a market system. In fact, if we are to understand how the system works, we need to consider the interactions between and among all the parties and elements that comprise it. For example, we can consider school boards, school administrators and teacher unions as elements of a coalition that "produces" education. We know that these parties are usually able to disseminate their point of view by means of news releases, news conferences and even, on occasion, advertising. Now ask yourself how frequently and how effectively the media articulate consumer interests. Do media allow the producers to pose successfully as consumer representatives? Are media even aware that this is or may be a critical public policy issue? If media purportedly represent consumer interests, how well prepared are reporters and editors to fulfill this role?

Let me illustrate the importance of these questions with a simple but striking example. By all accounts, *A Nation at Risk* was the most widely publicized and most influential educational reform report of the 1980s. The report was sponsored by the National Commission on Excellence in Education, an 18-member commission appointed by then-Secretary of Education Terrel H. Bell. The report was released in April 1983, and hundreds of thousands of copies were distributed by the federal government. The report, or major portions of it, were reprinted in the *New York Times* and other leading print media. *A Nation at Risk* was the main topic of discussion at thousands of education conventions and conferences, and virtually every leading journal of opinion for a lay audience published one or more commentaries on it. Professional journals invariably devoted a great deal of attention to it, as did educational organizations generally.

Despite this massive celebratory coverage, one key aspect of the report received virtually no press attention: *A Nation at Risk* was a unanimous report. It was unanimous because the commission members agreed in advance that it should be, and inasmuch as the commission included partisans or representatives of every major educational interest group, the unanimity policy precluded inclusion of any recommendation that posed a threat to any of these groups. Surely there is a world of difference between saying, "This is what we believe should be done to improve American education," and "This is what we believe should be done to improve American education, excluding all issues on which we do not have unanimous agreement among commission members." By not making any recommendations on issues lacking unanimity, *A Nation at Risk* concerned itself only with cosmetic issues, or pie-in-the-sky proposals on important ones. Not surprisingly, the report resulted in no significant change despite the enormous media attention it received.

Indeed, the most remarkable aspect of the report and its aftermath was the complete absence of any media attention to the reasons for unanimity and the consequences certain to follow from it. The reason for the unanimity approach was not stated but was hardly a mystery — the report was intended to generate political support, and you do not generally do that by antagonizing influential interest groups on truly important issues. Had even a handful of education reporters — perhaps only one in a major national newspaper or news magazine — expressed cognizance of the rationale for and implications of the unanimity, our nation might have been spared a tremendous amount of irrelevant discussion and debate. More importantly, we might not have been diverted from the real problems that must be faced to effect reform.

If this analysis seems unduly negative, consider the current wave of reform rhetoric on "restructuring" education. As is evident from events in the Soviet Union, real perestroika requires that various interest groups lose some of their advantages and prerogatives. Without some real pain, "restructuring" is only a harmless buzzword. Nonetheless, everyone in education claims to support "restructuring." Apparently if there are to be losers they will always be some other interest group. Meanwhile the news media are not just observing the debacle; by their witless reporting of "restructuring" statements, conferences and actions, they are helping mightily to create it.

The examples I've discussed here suggest several significant issues concerning the interrelationships between media and education. For instance, what proportion of educational news originates with education producers such as school boards, teacher unions and state departments of education? What proportion originates with or is devoted to consumer interests? What is the level of reportorial/editorial sophistication about educational issues? Is there any difference in reporting that can be attributed to the fact that some educational reporters (presumably) have studied educational policy, school finance or educational research? What correlation is there, if any, between the educational importance of an issue and the attention media devote to it? Is Lieberman's Law applicable here?

My comments thus far may be challenged for being too simplistic. "Media," of course, covers an enormous variety of dissemination networks: television, radio, newspapers, magazines and book publishing, to cite the most obvious. Each of these categories can in turn be divided in various ways that might affect an objective assessment of the treatment it accords elementary and secondary education. The national newspapers, for example, have reporters and editors who specialize in education news and analysis, and one might expect that such papers would display a higher level of educational sophistication than others that do not devote similar resources to the topic. This point may be valid as far as it goes, but it may not go far enough. Although I have what may be regarded as a rather low opinion of the sophistication of education reporters and editors, I do not believe that our nation's poor educational information system can be written off to deficient personnel policies. In any case, the wide disparities in educational sophistication among different media may be largely irrelevant to the origins of or the solution to our educational information problems.

Consider, for instance, the fact that education reporters frequently play a critical role in shaping educational policy, especially at the local level, and often in ways that they themselves do not fully appreciate. This is especially apparent in teacher strikes. Teacher salaries and benefits usually consume 50 percent to 75 percent of school budgets. On the other hand, teacher bargaining contracts govern the way teachers' work is regulated. The contracts cover assignment, courseload, transfers, evaluation procedures, class size, dismissal and discipline, and several other matters categorized as "terms and conditions of employment." Although the news media focus on salaries and fringe benefits, teacher bargaining contracts are extremely important policy documents. In effect, they provide the framework under which most expenditures are made.

A teacher strike is essentially a battle for public opinion. It may be a battle over money, but popular opinion, not economic pressure, is usually the decisive factor in resolving strikes. It would be difficult to overestimate the influence of media in these situations. In my 25 years of experience in school labor relations, I would have to say that reportorial sophistication about labor relations, or lack thereof, was a wild card — such that my own conclusion is that editorial competence is a much more serious problem than bias. Bias for one party or another certainly exists, but the bias itself often results from an incompetent analysis of the issues. I was often unpleasantly surprised by how easy it is to manipulate media coverage in teacher bargaining situations. Eventually I realized that I enjoyed similar opportunities, and I did not hesitate to take advantage of them in certain situations.

I mention strike situations primarily to underscore a critical but widely neglected aspect of media treatment of education: Educational issues often have economic or political dimensions, and a realistic evaluation of our educational information system has to take into account media sophistication and treatment of several "non-educational" issues. A reporter who is very knowledgeable about education, for instance, may unwittingly misinform and mislead a community because of a lack of sophistication on other issues — whether related to finances, law, race, religion or something else — a problem made worse by the fact that so many news media see the education beat merely as a training ground for some sexier billet.

Teacher salaries, to which the media devote enormous attention, provide an interesting illustration of this point. According to a 1990 publication of the U.S. Department of Education, the average teacher salary for the 1989–90 school year was $31,304. The publication goes on to say that "this represents an increase of 5.9 percent, in current dollars, over the revised figure of $29,547 in 1988–89."

How did the department come up with its figures? It did not conduct the research on salaries itself; instead it relied on the estimates of the National Education Association (NEA), the nation's largest teacher union. The department has followed this practice for several decades. Likewise, the news media rely almost exclusively on the NEA for salary data, and by doing so they mislead as well as misinform the American people about teacher compensation. Salary figures alone omit the dollar value of teacher fringe benefits: contributions to teacher pensions, health and dental insurance; a wide variety of leave benefits (sick, sabbatical, parental, adoption, military, union business, and so on); extra duty pay (coaching, band, school paper, student clubs, etc.); and workmen's compensation. These fringe benefits greatly exceed those paid to private school teachers, and in some states their dollar value is more than one-third of straight salary. Quite often news releases about teacher salaries include comparisons with other professions. The comparisons do not mention the fact that teachers work only 180 days a year on the average, and that their workday is less than in most full-time positions. It also overlooks a variety of benefits, such as teacher tenure and layoff and re-employment rights that are not available to most private sector employees. These benefits often impose direct and indirect costs on school districts, but do not show up as a benefit in the summaries of teacher compensation.

What reasons do the NEA (and the American Federation of Teachers) give for not including data on fringe benefits in its annual survey of teacher salaries? One is that it would be too expensive to get the data. The other is that private sector employees also receive fringe benefits, so the comparisons aren't really misleading. Both reasons do not survive examination. The NEA has extensive data on benefits but does not release them; and private sector employees do receive fringe benefits, though usually much less than what public employees get. This is especially true of teachers; not only are private school teachers paid lower salaries, but their fringe benefits tend to be even less attractive as a proportion of total compensation.

In my view the resolution of information issues will be among the two or three most critical factors affecting the future of American education in the coming years. To appreciate their importance, consider the information argument made by proponents of a voucher system, to wit, that parents need to know only which school is better for their children. Anyone facing such a choice can safely ignore most of the education issues that currently receive media attention. When we buy an automobile, we do not usually inquire about the manufacturer's management structure, the extent of employee turnover, or whether management utilizes a system of merit pay. We compare automobiles and choose. We look to *Consumer Reports*, not to the business section of the *New York Times* or network television news, if we need information and advice. If our practice in education were similar, parents would need information concerning the educational service from which they would choose. Information about career ladders, merit pay, school-based management and the plethora of policies associated with the management of public education would fade dramatically in importance.

Whether or not the comparison to a market system is valid, it suggests an imposing burden of proof on the information system currently associated with public education. The burden is to show that this system results in parent and taxpayer ability to monitor and adjust and appropriately restructure public schools. I doubt whether the news media, even in conjunction with information received directly from schools or community sources, can meet this burden, but my doubts are of secondary importance. What is primarily important is that the information issues be addressed in a more critical way, in both media and the field of education.

Myron Lieberman was a visiting scholar at the Social Philosophy and Policy Center, Bowling Green State University, Bowling Green, Ohio.

PART I

Education in the Media

2

The Twilight Zone Beat

Lawrence T. McGill

Public education in the United States is a $300 billion industry. Virtually every child in the country from the ages of 5 to 17 attends a school of one sort or another, and American educational institutions directly touch the lives of nearly every citizen at some point, most for more than a decade, many for nearly two decades or more. Professors and teachers perennially rate at or near the top of everyone's list of most admired professionals.

But news of education often seems to get lost in the shuffle. Indeed, the status of education as news was so tenuous at one point that in 1962 the *Saturday Review* published an article entitled simply, "Is Education News?" In the early 1980s, Mary Ellen Schoonmaker, former education writer at the *Record* in Bergen County, New Jersey, posed the dilemma in these terms:

> Somewhere in the collective unconscious of American journalism is the recognition that education ought to be seriously covered. In fact, it isn't. Editors send a small army of mostly underequipped, overworked and unencouraged reporters, many of whom view the beat as an obligatory period in purgatory, to cover a complex, elusive and challenging topic.

> Perhaps this schizophrenic attitude reflects America's odd stance toward education. This is the country, after all, that will someday send a teacher as the first private citizen into space—a reminder, says President Reagan, "of the crucial role teachers and education play in the life of our nation." Yet this is a country that, in 1983, paid teachers an average starting salary of $12,000 a year. The words and the music don't fit.

Anticipating the launch of the ill-fated space shuttle which carried teacher Christa McAuliffe, this quote illustrates a peculiar irony of education coverage, for which the explosion of the Challenger serves as a bitter, yet apt, metaphor. For the most part, what generally takes place every day in educational institutions (that is, teaching and learning) is not considered news. As pollster George Gallup put it:

> The media are prone to limit their coverage of news of the schools to what journalists describe as "spot" news—happenings or events that take place in the schools. Unfortunately, these stories usually concern vandalism, drugs, absenteeism, theft of school property, attacks on teachers and the like. "Good news" is difficult to find and report. Consequently, the public receives a distorted picture of schools and tends to regard them as blackboard jungles.

Adds Nat Hentoff of the *Village Voice*, "[It's news] when something happens at the top of the pyramid. The basic denial of the tools children need to get somewhere is not news." Dennis Doyle, as director of Education Policy Studies at the American Enterprise Institute, wrote that, as a rule, two themes tend to predominate in the coverage of education:

> First is education as ceremony and honor. . . . These are the "feel good" news stories that fill space as they permit achievers to be honored and get some local names into the paper. Interestingly enough, these stories are almost never accompanied by any analysis—they are straight description. . . .
>
> The second education "story" is education as politics and theatre, education as a process of competition for scarce resources and as a stage upon which actors strut. In this case, substantive issues fall by the wayside. The education story becomes a recap of the most recent outburst at the school board meeting, disputes about busing, arguments over school closings, debates about football eligibility, strikes and labor-management disputes, real or imagined. Not far behind are the stories with lurid details about assaults on teachers or students, child abuse, drugs on campus, and guns in the hall.

Some editors, though, turn this lack of substantive focus on teaching and learning into a plus rather than a minus, pointing out that the coverage of "education" means dealing with issues that cut across many other important news areas. Saundra Keyes of the *Orlando Sentinel* notes that education coverage provides reporters the opportunity to deal with such topics as:

- *Politics*, in selection of superintendents, allocation of tax dollars, and legislation on issues ranging from competency testing to how much time students should spend in class;

- *Religion*, school prayer and church-state separation;

- *Business*, how well vocational education programs serve local employers; school-business partnerships in computer training and other areas;

- *Courts*, school-related litigation; links between the juvenile justice system and education;

- *Sports*, academic requirements for athletes;

- *Race relations*, desegregation; representation of minority students in classes for high and low achievers;

- *Social issues*, sex education and teenage pregnancy; effects of single-parent homes on school performance.

The problem with this argument is its implicit suggestion that the primary value of working on the education beat is that it prepares a reporter to move on to more prestigious topics as he or she moves up the career ladder. Indeed, research shows this tends to be the case.

To obtain information on the beat structure at U.S. dailies, the Freedom Forum Media Studies Center commissioned a study of U.S. newspaper editors in which the top editors at nearly 300 papers participated. Among other things, we asked them to provide information about the staffing of different beats, to identify the topics that appeared most frequently on the front page of their papers, to rate news beats in terms of importance and status, and to assess the role that beat experiences played in helping to advance their careers. The findings from this study reflect, in many ways, the ambivalent feelings toward education coverage discussed above.

Allocation of personnel. In total, there are probably about 1,600 reporters covering the education beat at U.S. dailies (of which there were about 1,550 in 1986), making it the sixth largest beat overall. The sports beat is the largest, with nearly four-and-a-half times as many reporters covering sports as education.

Obviously it is unreasonable to expect education coverage at smaller papers to look the same as education coverage at larger papers, and so in our study we grouped U.S. dailies into four size categories — large (circulation over 100,000), medium (circulation between 50,000 and 100,000), small (circulation between 10,000 and 50,000) and tiny (circulation below 10,000). In general, based on data provided by the editors who participated in this study, we estimate that the average number of reporters on staff at tiny papers is about 10, at small papers about 18, at medium papers about 35, and at large papers about 106.

The proportion of the news staff assigned to the coverage of education varies from about 6 percent at the smallest papers to about 2.5 percent at the largest.

An education reporter at the smallest papers will typically spend about half of his or her time covering education and half covering other news. But because the total reporting staff is so small, the proportionate emphasis on education at the smallest papers is greater than at the largest ones. At papers with circulations above 100,000, the reporting staff is more than 10 times as large, but the total number of education reporters on staff is larger by a factor of only about 4 or 5. The sports staff, by comparison, is larger by a factor of more than 15.

So what happens is that at the largest papers education coverage tends to get lost among the coverage given to other topics, whose beats have expanded faster as papers get larger. Conversely, there is a perception among editors that the education beat is actually quite strong at smaller papers in the United States. As Christopher Connell, former education reporter for the Washington bureau of the Associated Press, notes, it is "astonishing how often you find [small and medium-sized] newspapers running big, front-page, lead stories on education."

Connell's observation tends to be supported, in fact, by the data we collected in our survey of editors. While virtually no editors said that education was *the* most frequent front-page story at their paper, it was listed as one of the top *four* front-page stories by about 30 percent of editors at papers with circulations under 50,000 (ranking 6th out of 18 topics). Fewer editors at medium-sized papers listed education as one of the top four front-page stories (17 percent; ranking 9th), and fewer still at large papers (9 percent; also ranking 9th).

Not surprisingly, political coverage tends to appear on the front page of the newspaper more often than any other kind of news, regardless of the size of the paper. Three-quarters of the editors surveyed named news of local, national, or state government and politics as the type of story that appears most frequently on their front pages. Local government and politics came in first (45 percent of editors rank it number 1), followed by national government and politics (26 percent). Business and economy came in a distant third (8 percent).

Aside from these three topics, two others appear on the front pages of small and tiny newspapers more often than education: disasters and accidents, and police and crime. At medium and large papers, international news, state government and politics, and social issues also rank ahead of education as front-page topics. The net effect of the redistribution of staff across beats and changes in the composition of the front page at these larger, more influential newspapers is that education coverage assumes a steadily smaller and less prominent place in their news mix.

Importance of coverage. Strikingly, despite the fact that education ranks sixth in terms of the number of reporters covering the beat, and eighth overall as a front-page topic, editors rank it higher in importance than any other beat. Overall, out of a list of 18 beats, editors rated education either *the* most important or second most important beat at papers with circulations under 100,000, and the fifth most important at larger papers. On a scale of 1 to 5 (with 1 indicating "very low importance" and 5 "very high importance"), not a single editor assigned education an importance rating of less than 3. No other beat was skewed so unanimously in a positive direction.

Close behind education in importance are sports, local government and politics, and business and the economy. These four beats plus police and crime coverage are listed by editors as the five most important beats at papers with circulations below 50,000. At circulations above 50,000, these four plus arts, culture and entertainment are considered the most important beats to cover (police and crime coverage having dropped out of the top 10 entirely).

While editors consider education, sports, and business and economic news to be as important as news of government and politics, the front page is nevertheless clearly dominated by the latter. It's no mystery why sports isn't on the front page, having its own section, and business news may not appear as frequently there for the same reason. But education, ranked by editors as *the* most important area of coverage overall, fails to show up among the top five categories of news stories most frequently appearing on the front page of newspapers of all sizes.

Such a discrepancy between avowed "importance" and frequency of appearance on page one suggests a clear selection bias at work in the organization of the news. One interpretation might be that although the coverage of politics and education are in fact equally vital, the press views itself as having a special mandate to cover politics above all other topics. Indeed, there is merit to this perspective, but it could also mean that education news is grossly undervalued by journalists as front-page copy, in spite of their general agreement as to its importance. The staffing practices at newspapers lend support to the latter premise, since on a typical paper with a circulation over 100,000, education reporters tend to account for only 2 or 3 people out of a staff of more than 100, while political reporters account for about 13.

Status of the beat. The status of a particular news beat is a different kind of measure than importance: Simply put, status is more likely to be related to a reporter's opportunities for career advancement. For example, editors list sports and education as the topics that are most important to cover, and yet it would come as a surprise if either of these beats provided more or greater career advancement opportunities than the political beat. In fact, education in particular has been traditionally deprecated as a beat almost antithetical to career advancement. *Time* magazine writer William A. Henry III, speaking of his experiences in newspaper journalism, says, "It was assumed, indeed it was said outright to me, that an ambitious young man would not expect to stay long on the education beat. . . . And as my editors had predicted, I lasted on the beat about nine months before moving on (and in their view, up)."

At first glance, the education beat seems to do quite well, coming in fourth *overall* in terms of the relative status conferred by the coverage of different beats. But this is deceptive because the status of the education beat drops dramatically as papers get larger: Education ranks third in status at tiny papers (behind local government/politics and sports), but drops to fifth at small papers, eighth at medium papers, and finally to 12th at the largest papers.

The effect of beat experiences on journalists' career paths. What probably overrides almost all other considerations affecting journalists' opinions about the education beat are their beliefs about how best to get ahead in their careers. Although for editors "experiences on a particular beat" rank fourth among nine factors contributing to their professional success, it's likely that career reporters should find beat experiences even more important.

Among editors, the political beat was mentioned more often than any other as the beat that made a difference in their careers. It was mentioned five times as often as the second most frequently mentioned beat — sports — and more than nine times as often as education. Experiences on the education beat played an important role in the careers of just 2 percent of the editors in our survey, despite the fact that more than half of them reported having spent some time on the beat at some point in their career.

This probably implies not so much a devaluing of the education beat as it does a strong positive valuation of the political beat: It is through the coverage of those with power that journalists gain power for themselves. In her book *Making News* sociologist Gaye Tuchman notes that "the higher the status of sources and the greater the scope of their positions, the higher the status of the reporters. As is well known, news stories, news sources and reporters are hierarchically arranged."

In our society, the coverage of the powerful means the coverage of politics. Add to this the generally accepted characterization of the press as the fourth branch of government and you have a powerful ideological context that supports the notion that the political beat is the place to be. Indeed, in surveys of journalists, "investigating government claims" appears time and again as the one aspect of their role in American society with which journalists most strongly agree. Given all of this, it is not surprising that journalists who ply the education beat typically view it as little more than a steppingstone in their careers.

Content analyses of the evening news programs of the three broadcast networks paint a picture of education coverage very similar to that of United States daily newspapers. According to Andrew D. Tyndall, editor of the *Tyndall Report* and president of Tyndall Research, education ranked 13th out of 18 topics tracked on the network newscasts in 1990, receiving a total of 368 minutes of coverage across the three newscasts. This works out to an average of just a little over 10 minutes per newscast per month, or about 2.2 percent of all newstime (which is quite comparable to the 2.5 percent of all reporters at the largest U.S. dailies assigned to the education beat). To place education coverage on the network newscasts in some kind of context, the level of coverage given to education in 1990 was comparable to the levels of coverage given to such topics as transportation and accidents (2.6 percent), sports (2.5 percent), natural disasters (2.3 percent), and issues of race and immigration (2.1 percent).

Needless to say, coverage of war and the threat of war accounted for the largest proportion of network news coverage in 1990 — about 21 percent of it. Although war-related stories received more than twice as much coverage as 1989's number one topic received (business, finance and the economy — 8.4 percent), this extra emphasis on war did not take away from the coverage of education in 1990. In fact, network newscast coverage of education was up 23 percent from 1989 (when it ranked 16th out of 18 categories), and up 87 percent from 1988 (when it ranked 18th, behind even coverage of "animals"!).

ABC, which Tyndall has dubbed the "education network," has set the pace in boosting education coverage. The network's "World News Tonight" has found a place for semi-regular education coverage in its "American Agenda" feature, a social-concerns segment that appears in almost every newscast. "NBC Nightly News" recently instituted a set of regular segments in its newscast that have provided a venue for education-related stories, especially in its "What Works" feature, which focuses on innovative solutions to social problems. What is most notable about this particular feature is that its solution-oriented focus has allowed educational "success" stories to find their way into the newscast.

One thing that most people in the news business seem to agree on is that the current public demand for news about and related to education is high. Christopher Peck, managing editor of the *Spokane Spokesman-Review*, indicates that "education coverage has become in the last year or two a much higher-interest item to our readers. . . . Education's a really hot topic right now, so we're going to be devoting more resources to it." Audience surveys conducted by the major television networks confirm these high levels of interest in education news.

While it is true that the main structural impediment to improving education coverage (namely, the journalistic career system) is unlikely ever to be completely overcome, there are in the meantime some concrete steps that players on both sides of the education fence can take to effect improvements. For journalists to be able to cover the beat as the public requires, they must first come to a clearer understanding of the American educational institution. And in somewhat ironic but parallel fashion, educators and educational administrators must themselves be educated about the nature and workings of the press.

With respect to reporters, Roger Yarrington, the former associate dean of the University of Maryland College of Journalism, suggests that "reporters covering education must have a knowledge of the history of education and how it is organized and financed if they are going to do a quality job." He further suggests that both "pre-service" and "in-service" training and enrichment programs be instituted, which "should include exposure to successful practitioners and courses [in education], . . . probably at the M.A. level."

Journalist Larry Hayes offers a comprehensive prescription for improvement on the journalistic side of the relationship:

> Observe classes. Reporters rarely do. Editorial writers don't. So we describe what people say about classes or schools or universities. It's like doing archaeology by reading comic books on dinosaurs.

> . . . . You've got to support your people. Give them time for that reading, send them to conferences like Education Writers Association programs and let them visit universities to talk with a variety of people about teaching—not just in education departments, either.

> . . . . Report the minimum test scores and minimum standards and how much television has ruined all our minds, if you must. But I beg you also to look to the real story. It's a human tragedy that's going on right under our noses every time a kid is told he's just average, or can't really learn anything hard or that he ought to be ashamed for putting the comma in the wrong place.

An even simpler suggestion for improvement comes from Wilma Morrison, former education editor at the Portland *Oregonian*: "Give more space to a school story than would be given to a story of comparable importance about another public agency. A lot of misinterpretations and falsifications that raise holy hob with public schools come not from intent to deceive but from excessive brevity."

Larry Hayes leaves us with one final irony to ponder concerning this most paradoxical of institutional relationships. Rhetorically he asks, "Did you know that teachers and school officials and parents almost never read research on education? You know what they read? Your newspapers. Don't let them down."

Lawrence T. McGill is manager, news audience research, at NBC and was a 1987 research fellow at The Freedom Forum Media Studies Center at Columbia University.

3

Oh, When I Was Young!

George R. Kaplan

Of the diverse media voices capable of shaping public opinion on the schools, columns by journalists of national reputation may be the most disappointing. The pundits rarely bother with public education. Given a choice between commenting on Bulgarian economic prospects or a revolutionary development affecting inner city schools, their decision on a topic for 800 words of solemn pontification is foreordained. The Bulgarians would win in a walk.

Syndicated columnists impart a kind of intellectual respectability to editorial and op-ed pages and, occasionally, to TV news and public affairs programs. Whatever their philosophical bent, they are for the most part worldly men (most *are* men) with wide-ranging interests and a superior grasp of the forces and processes that drive public policy. They are consummately literate and can synthesize complex ideas in expressive yet succinct language. They delight in absorbing new, unexamined information. Many are unabashed fact-blotters with an enviable knack for enlisting data in the service of ideology. To readers in many communities, nationally syndicated columns are a welcome change from the otherwise insipid editorial fare of their local newspapers.

When it comes to education, though, most columnists are unembarrassed traditionalists. When they do comment, as during the "education summit" in Charlottesville, Virginia, in September 1989, the drift of their analysis is numbingly predictable. The normally pervasive matter of political orientation recedes, and an idealized mental image of schools as they used to be, or as the writers choose to remember them, takes over. Whether liberal or conservative, their commentary is a set piece. The villains are school bureaucracies, the erosion of such fundamental values as discipline and homework, and a core of supposedly incompetent teachers. To our op-ed page analysts, educational reform customarily means dragging the schools back a half-century as rapidly as possible. If old-fashioned, no-nonsense schools worked for them, why shouldn't they succeed for today's children?

While this familiar litany has some appeal, it is a largely unconsidered reaction. It simply ignores decades of breakthroughs in many sectors of education as well as sea changes in demography and social policy. The opinion columnist who interviews a dozen sources and reads 150 pages of from-the-scene reporting before composing a piece on, say, the U.S. negotiating stance on military bases in the Philippines, will blithely unleash a fiery blast against the schools with almost no briefing or current factual background. Education is like politics, sex and baseball; we are certain that we know all there is to know.

Perversely, this lack of thoughtful commentary may not be an altogether bad thing. If the columnists were to write often and knowledgeably about the schools, education's spokespersons might find themselves in a real bind. All but a few of public education's defenders would be out of their league in verbal or literary confrontations with the nation's think-piece artisans. They would be hard put, for example, to refute charges that student achievement has wobbled or that violence in the schools is rising. Besides, the probability that a rare shot at the schools by a Tom Wicker or a William F. Buckley Jr. (who have boatloads of other fish to fry) would cause an immediate ruckus in state legislatures or governors' offices probably ranges from zero to negligible. To the big-name pundits, the most explosive educational issue imaginable would probably not score 2.3 on a journalistic Richter scale.

It does rankle, though, that so many nominal supporters of a sensible, proactive social policy tend to be as unthinkingly harsh on the schools as their less charitable peers. To take one example, David Broder, the dean of America's political columnists and one of the few who have begun to worry in print about education, has peppered his syndicated columns with tough, sometimes excessive criticism of the schools. After a refreshing burst of candor — when he correctly labeled former Secretary of Education William Bennett the James Watts of the second Reagan term — Broder consistently identified himself with Bennett's loose-cannon assaults and left little doubt that he favored returning schools to the good old days when he was a student (probably a superior one against difficult odds).

By most reasonable measures, the situation of the schools should be a topic of regular discussion by the media's more cerebral analysts. Some readers may deem it even more newsworthy than flag burning or Imelda Marcos. But that is not the case, nor has it been for a generation or more, or perhaps ever. Even in the golden age of newspaper columns, when the work of a relatively small number of stars such as Walter Lippmann, Dorothy Thompson (who did write about the schools from time to time), Marquis Childs, and a bit later, Arthur Krock and Drew Pearson, was devoured by a public still free of the spell of television, the schools were virtually off-limits. In those days, though, the reasons for bypassing them were infinitely nobler than today's rationales. It was an accepted article of American faith that public education was the very foundation of our successful experiment in democracy. Not only was it doing its job — usually with underpaid teachers, overcrowded classrooms, and dictatorial administrators — but it was doing it with distinction. This granitic verity evoked such a powerful consensus that even the most responsible critical commentary would have been considered heretical. Many observant Americans sensed that much was wrong and that the role of non-school factors was greatly underestimated, but the burden of analysis stayed largely within the profession.

Today's most widely syndicated columnists can choose from a smorgasbord of subjects. With scattered exceptions, though, they have become captives of the priorities of political administrations. In practice, this means that they share the fixation with politics and national security that has dominated every presidency since Franklin Roosevelt's. Unlike domestic social policy, the realm of international affairs offers the possibility of exotic travel and the prospect of witnessing history in the making. Some journalists have even become part of it. Far from least, commenting on events beyond our borders furnishes an opportunity to work in an area that permits huge margins for error. When the tensions of foreign policy lift, the elite columnists usually have a political aftermath to analyze. And when that ebbs, the chronically troubled economy or even the environment beckons for attention.

Whatever their message may be and whether they deserve it or not (most do), columnists are read, seen and heard by the nation's decision-makers and, almost equally important, their gurus and gatekeepers. It is less clear today how respectful their reception may be. Some, such as Broder, impart instant legitimacy to an issue or cause. William Raspberry's incisive comments on social issues command immediate respect in Washington's decision-making circles. Certainly there has never been another columnist of the stature of Lippmann, who advised nearly every president from Theodore Roosevelt to Lyndon Johnson and actually drafted Woodrow Wilson's Fourteen Points, or of Joseph Alsop, whose ardent espousal of U.S. intervention in Vietnam may have been a crucial element in persuading his friend John F. Kennedy to commit American forces. There is reason to suspect that their impact at the stratified level has weakened substantially since the Nixon administration, although Will was a Reagan confidant of sorts and lunched periodically with the First Lady.

The columnists nevertheless remain an acknowledged body of attention-compelling sages whose long-term influence on a concerned citizenry and its political leaders may be unmatched by any other group in public communication. A national leader would be unwise to ignore the imposing presence of the *New York Times*'s William Safire. Right or wrong, the avowedly conservative Safire is a thoroughly informed thinker with great sources and a superb mastery of the issues. It almost goes without saying that he has paid no serious attention to the schools. Nor have Will, Wicker, Jack Anderson, Anthony Lewis or all but a tiny handful of their fellow seers.

The prospect that the institution of the syndicated column will focus its formidable intellectual energy on education as it does on other public issues is far from bright. Most of the columnists are moderate to conservative middle-aged white men — at a time when the schools of our cities are serving a swiftly expanding population of poor children of color. Such female columnists as Ellen Goodman, Anna Quindlen and Mary McGrory do devote responsible thought and countless column inches to social concerns, but their enlightened opinions are too seldom discernible in the cacophony created by their male peers. Little or nothing is heard on such themes from Jeane Kirkpatrick, Meg Greenfield or Flora Lewis.

This is no small shortcoming. Despite the overwhelming preponderance of female teachers and the strong presence of woman reporters on the education beat throughout the country, the female approach to communication — generally constructive and cooperative, non-threatening and empathetic — is not usually to be found in the national columns when education or children's issues are featured. The nation's readers are the losers. The educational atavism of the big-name male columnists may have its place, but it badly needs to be counter-balanced by the more relevant insights of journalism's best female analysts. A greatly broadened dissemination of the twice-weekly columns of the *New York Times*'s Anna Quindlen would be a splendid start. Women, says Deborah Tannen, the author of *You Just Don't Understand: Women and Men in Communications*, "tend to use language to create intimacy and connections." These are underplayed when journalism's wise men turn to stories on human needs and social institutions. Only Colman McCarthy lobbies consistently for person-based rather than budget-driven policies.

Within their own cosmos, the several million people who work in education are similarly underexposed to policy-oriented editorial commentary. Hundreds of national, regional and state education organizations, as well as a large collection of private publishers, regurgitate a limitless array of magazines, journals and newsletters. The quality and looks of some, such as *Teacher* and *Principal*, would do honor to any profession. Columnists abound throughout this self-contained constellation, but their output normally centers on the bread-and-butter issues of immediate concern to their specialized professional constituencies. Of the three principal all-purpose national education publications — *Education Week*, the *Chronicle of Higher Education* and the monthly *Phi Delta Kappan* — only the latter, with approximately 150,000 mostly influential subscribers and a large pass-along readership of teachers and education leaders, has seen fit to provide space for broadly based editorial opinion. Anne Lewis's monthly *Kappan* column from Washington provides a top-notch analyst's insights into current and emerging issues. It merits syndication beyond the field.

Any assessment of the ultimate place of the pundits must hinge on their recent record. Have they offered a conceptual backdrop that merits the respect of decision-makers? Do they have insights that a public figure's inner circle of advisers and information sources might lack? Can they help concerned readers make up their minds about important public matters? More bluntly, have they been right or wrong most of the time?

That the journalistic experts are often brilliant in their analysis of the top of the news is indisputable. Far less certain is their overall performance record. In presidential politics, for example, few believed it possible, even conceivable when their primary campaigns began, that

Richard Nixon ("You won't have Nixon to kick around any more," after his defeat in the 1962 California gubernatorial campaign), Jimmy Carter (1976), or Ronald Reagan (1976) would make it to the White House except as dinner guests. The gravity of the savings and loan debacle blew by the oblivious or otherwise engaged pundits even as its dimensions seemed to be expanding geometrically. The 1989 revolutions in a half-dozen East European countries came as a surprise to virtually every columnist in American journalism. Only an unknown British observer, Timothy Garton Ash, in a series of astonishing reports in the *New York Review of Books*, spotted the imminent collapse of the totalitarian regimes. But Ash's route to his riveting forecasts would be anathema to most of his American colleagues. He learned the languages, cultivated close and sometimes dangerous ties with the emerging leaders, and read everything he could get his hands on long before chaos descended.

Education's tale belongs on the endless list of stories missed and trends misread. It may be too much to hope that journalism's megastars will weigh in sensibly on what has been happening in and to the schools. But it is conceivable that the pronouncements of the media's best and brightest would spark a genuine public debate on public education. No one has yet snapped at the bait. In the right hands, the admittedly slow-moving story of change in the schools could become an absorbing and productive specialty.

The absence of a focused national column on education worsens the already severe problem of inadequate information-sharing by schools and education professionals. Since well before the establishment in the early 1970s of the now-disbanded National Institute of Education, which had the unenviable task of disseminating applicable research findings, the U.S. government and the teachers' unions have had indifferent success in promoting the adoption of "the best of educational practice" by the nation's schools. The word gets out to school districts through the small, well-managed National Diffusion Network and such primer-level publications as the Department of Education's *What Works*. Though anecdotal evidence suggests that they reach some of their targets some of the time, these materials are only technically in the public domain. For the most part, they are simply a trickle in the flood of paper that crosses the typical district school superintendent's desk. Rarely do they command the attention of parents or the larger public. Even the weekly columns by Albert Shanker, which originate as paid advertisements in the Sunday *New York Times* and are picked up gratis by 60 to 80 additional newspapers, do not appear to have made much of a dent beyond the large circle of educators who admire the high intelligence he invariably displays.

It is a large leap from officially disseminated research data, some of it obvious and repetitive, and subsidized columns by teacher union leaders to the musings of big-time national pundits. And when the columnists take time out from politics and national security to examine social problems, they can hardly be expected to expostulate on the advantages of more homework or of parents reading to their children, two of the banalities of *What Works*. Instead they tend to dilate on such topics as the sinister economic meaning of the latest results of the National Assessment of Educational Progress, or violence, drug use and immorality among high school children.

"If politicians are to be able to decide what the electorate wants," says media chronicler Jude Wanniski, "they have to have the parameters of the debate communicated to them by the scriveners." This has yet to happen in education. Literally and symbolically, the columnists are failing to get at what ails elementary and secondary education — and what is still good about it. Their infrequent acknowledgement of the nation's 45 million school children is perfunctory and poorly informed. They do a disservice to our schools and to our children.

George R. Kaplan is a Washington-based writer on leadership, educational policy and the media. Most recently he is the author of *Images of Education: The Mass Media's Version of America's Schools*.

4

Reading, Writing, and Taxes

Jim Edgar

It is ritualistic for gubernatorial candidates in Illinois to declare education as their top priority, and because they do, it rarely becomes a pivotal issue in a campaign for our state's highest office. But 1990 was different. Education did become a pivotal issue in both the primary and general elections for governor of Illinois — because, in addition to engaging in the traditional rhetoric about education, I also said throughout my campaign that I would favor continuation of an income tax surcharge to assure adequate funding for our schools.

In 1989 a Democratic-controlled General Assembly and Governor James R. Thompson, a Republican, had approved a temporary increase in the state income tax — from 2.5 percent to 3 percent for individuals and from 4 percent to 4.8 percent for corporations — to generate an additional $350 million for elementary, secondary and higher education, and another $350 million for local governments. The legislation set out a surcharge expiration date of July 1, 1991, which meant that the state's new governor would have to consider immediately after being inaugurated whether to fight for its continuation in the spring legislative session.

I knew that the educational needs prompting approval of the surcharge would not magically evaporate on July 1, 1991, and I decided that I should be candid with voters about my position on the tax before the election. However my position on the surcharge and my pro-choice stand on abortion prompted a primary challenge from a relative unknown, and, though I won the primary by nearly a 2-1 margin, several media commentators in the state interpreted the 32 percent showing by my opponent as a sign of my political vulnerability on the tax issue.

My own analysis, shared by the few media commentators who took the trouble to look closely at the returns, indicated that the abortion issue was the key factor in boosting my opponent above the 30 percent mark; on the heels of the U.S. Supreme Court decision in the *Webster* case, many people who had not previously voted in a Republican primary took GOP ballots to support my anti-choice challenger.

That's not the way the media read it, however, and the tax revolt spin prevailed. In fact, the surcharge issue was to become such a focal point for the media of our state that it was difficult for reporters to focus on anything else during the general election campaign — especially after my Democratic opponent, who had supported imposition of the surcharge, declared his opposition to extending it.

Other issues in the campaign generated comparatively scant coverage — although some reporters, especially those working for the print media, provided exceptions to the rule. My environmental views, for instance, received considerably more attention *after* the election, even though I spelled them out during a period in the campaign when coverage was most intense. The same was true for my views on economic development. And even in the education area only a few reporters took the trouble, the space and the time to compare and contrast the candidates' positions on the many important educational issues that went beyond the funding question.

For instance, although my opponent and I agreed that standards should be established for measuring the performance of schools, we disagreed sharply on what those standards should be. He placed far more emphasis on standardized test results, whereas I said factors such as how graduates of a high school performed in higher education and on the job should be given considerable weight, and that schools also should be judged on what they had done to increase parental involvement. Yet those differences and others got almost no attention. In fact, there was only spotty coverage of a comprehensive education reform package I proposed — a package called for such things as:

- Establishment of councils at the state and local levels that would bring together educators and business executives to help assure schools were producing the right results for the workplace.

- Special scholarships for minority students to encourage them to enter the teaching field, where they could become badly needed positive role models.

- Internship programs for top-ranking sophomores and juniors in our colleges and universities to provide early linkage between them and Illinois businesses so we could reverse the state's "brain drain."

- A major initiative to teach teachers how to use computers in the classroom so they and their students could adapt to and take advantage of technological change.

A central question raised by my gubernatorial campaign is this: In a nation where the education of our young people will be one of the most important concerns of the next decade, will the news media be willing to examine all the problems affecting education in depth, and especially within the context of campaigns for major public office? Even on the surcharge issue that dominated our campaign, much of the coverage was superficial. Many news media did little more than report that I advocated extension as the means to adequately maintain education funding, while my opponent was proposing funding of education through enactment of hundreds of millions of unspecified cuts in other programs.

My observations here should not be construed as a diatribe against the media. Many reporters share my concern for the limited amount of attention their editors and producers are willing (or competitively able) to devote to serious coverage and analysis of public policy issues during a campaign. Moreover I would be greatly remiss if I didn't point out that there were outstanding examples of thorough reporting that, among other things, did expose the fallacy of my opponent's contention that schools could be adequately funded without extending the surcharge.

I respect the work of those in the media who do devote considerable time, energy and attention to the great issues. In addition I appreciate the frustration of reporters, editors and producers who are constrained by the realities of trying to produce news reports that balance what the public needs to know with what titillates readers and viewers. I also appreciate that I garnered editorial endorsements from the vast majority of Illinois newspapers largely because of my candor on the extension issue. And, as I begin to govern in a state where the needs are great and the resources limited, I am glad that I spoke forthrightly as a candidate so I could govern more effectively as a chief executive. Education can truly be my top priority as governor because I took the risk of truly making it my priority as a candidate.

Jim Edgar is the governor of Illinois.

5

Title Goes Here*

John Merrow

ITEM: A popular reader for first graders tells the fable *The Tortoise and the Hare* without using the words "tortoise" or "hare."

ITEM: Virtually every household in America has a television set; there are now more than 176 million television sets in this country.

ITEM: The publishers of *American Adventure*, a seventh-grade history textbook, deleted the word "inalienable" from the Declaration of Independence because they felt the word was too difficult.

ITEM: The U.S. Coast Guard received two dozen letters and telegrams demanding that it send a ship to rescue the castaways from the U.S.S. *Minnow*. The alarmed citizens had seen the nautical accident on the television sitcom "Gilligan's Island."

ITEM: An actor on an afternoon soap opera received at least 10 letters warning him that his television wife was secretly having an affair with his television lawyer and that they were planning to kill him in an upcoming episode.

Anyone reading the preceding items would be hard pressed not to conclude that the country is going to hell in a handbasket. After all, the school curriculum is pabulum or worse, and everybody sits in front of the tube, believing what they see.

All that would seem to be left to argue about is the *cause* of our decline. Was it television's "cotton candy for the brain" that so numbed our thinking that publishers were forced to "dumb down" textbooks? Or were

---

* Articles about television and education generally pose a question in their titles: "Television: Education or Confusion? Bane or Blessing?" So I asked my editor to subtitle this effort "Threat or Menace?" But he refused.

the educators the first to slide into mediocrity, forcing television producers to "dumb down" their programs to a level that their poorly educated audience could understand?

Educators, quite naturally, are prone to accept the "cotton candy" analysis. Television is a "plug in drug" and a "wasteland" to boot, leaving schools with an impossible task.

Blaming schools or television for the other's failures is a classic case of *post hoc, ergo propter hoc*. The "after this, therefore because of this" fallacy is easy to succumb to, but well off the mark. Much of what is on television is admittedly mediocre, but for reasons that have little to do with schools. I also believe that the omnipresence of television is not a valid excuse for our schools' general failure to educate our children adequately.

Television is certainly a convenient whipping boy. It's a curious paradox that educators regard television, simultaneously, with awe and contempt. Widely acknowledged as the most powerful educational tool ever invented, television has almost from the beginning been derided as a "wasteland" and worse. How often have we heard prophets of doom bemoaning the fact that "by high school graduation, nearly all American children will have spent more hours in front of the tube than in a classroom." That lament is nearly always part of the explanation for poor student performance, i.e., "We did our best but we can't compete with television. It's an unfair fight."

The argument is full of holes. On the one hand, television is so seductive and compelling that our children sit and watch for hours. On the other hand, television is so simple and mind-numbing that our children are brain-damaged and can't learn effectively.

Yes, our children grow up spending more time watching TV than sitting in class. That is not a particularly surprising fact, given that our children spend only about 7.2 percent of their first 18 years in class. The average youngster spends five hours a day in class (not in school), 175 days a year, for 13 of those 18 years. That's 11,375 classroom hours. Watch an average of 1 hour and 45 minutes of TV every day for 18 years, and TV time exceeds classroom time. Since youngsters watch 2-3 hours of TV daily (probably less than their parents, by the way), yes, TV viewing does exceed classroom time.

But when school is in session, it occupies *more* hours of the day than does television. If one considers only the school-age years, 5 to 18, and also factors out the summers and weekends, then class time wins hands down over all but the extreme cases of couch potatoes. Few children watch five hours of television a day while school is in session, and that means that educators cannot use *quantity* of viewing as an explanation for school failure, in my opinion.

A more plausible explanation for school failure is school itself. That is, educators should consider what goes on *during school time*: the mind-numbing drills, tedious lectures, busywork, and fuzzy-minded "social development" exercises that replace challenging academic work. Educators should consider how little they ask of students, i.e., homework assignments. American students at every grade level are asked to do far less homework than their counterparts in other industrialized countries. In *What Our 17-Year-Olds Know*, Chester Finn and Diane Ravitch reveal that many *college-bound* high school students have about an hour of homework a night.

While we're on the subject of curriculum, here's an extra-credit quiz: What work of children's literature is this (revised) passage taken from? Hint: It's the opening paragraph.

> Tap, tap, tap. See me work. I make good things. See the red ones. See the blue ones. See the yellow ones. No, no, no, I do not want red ones. I do not want blue ones. I want green ones.*

What educators believe about *the purpose of schooling* may be more to the point than television's influence. Recently I moderated a discussion on PBS about effective education for young children. "Granted," I said, "that building students' self-esteem and challenging them academically are both important. But which takes precedence?" The discussion that followed was illuminating. One woman argued that true education begins with respect for the learner, which requires a challenging curriculum. "Self-esteem grows out of mastery of significant material," she said.

"No," answered another educator. "Boost their self-esteem by praising them, hugging them, and then they can learn." Most heads nodded agreement.

After some debate I asked for a vote. To my disbelief, 19 of the 20 educators voted for "self-esteem." Near-unanimity in favor of warm fuzzies says volumes about schooling today, in my judgment. If that

---

* It's from "The Shoemaker and the Elves." I'm not certain that those of you who got the answer deserve credit or sympathy.

pseudo-philosophy rules, then standard network fare might as well *be* the entire curriculum.

In other words, television is a scapegoat, an excuse rather than an explanation for poorly led, unfocused educational enterprises.

Happily there are enough exceptions to that conclusion. Many in education seek to use television as an adjunct to their curriculum. This occurs chiefly in two ways: videotapes in the classroom or "assigned viewing." The computer revolution notwithstanding, the VCR is still the technology of choice in America's classrooms. Teachers complement their curriculum with documentaries or taped lectures, or specialists provide instruction-cum-videotape on "good touching and bad touching" (child abuse), sexuality or individual differences. A third, newer approach: actual courses in television-watching, usually given some high-falutin name like "media literacy" or "critical viewing."

In my experience, group TV-watching is poor pedagogy. Conventional documentaries are too long at 30 or 60 minutes, and the screen is too small for at least half of the class. I've seen teachers interrupt the documentaries and (valiantly) try to get students to discuss or even to summarize what they've seen, but that generally comes off as patronizing or pointless.

"Assigned viewing" has a better chance of success. Every history teacher worth his or her salt certainly assigned "The Civil War," Ken Burns' PBS series. Savvy teachers regularly check the TV listings for opportunities to supplement their courses. In addition, networks like A&E, Discovery and the one I work for, The Learning Channel, have well-organized efforts to inform teachers of programs that might help their teaching.

Another form of assigned viewing is what one sixth-grade teacher I know calls "going with the flow." He knew his students watched "The Simpsons" and "ALF," and so he made them an assignment. One week his students had to write several paragraphs describing what one character did, and why. Another week students had to listen for, and keep a list of, adverbs. Another assignment had students keeping track of commercials and writing paragraphs explaining which they felt were best, and why.

Does that approach work? Of course it does, if the teacher reads the paragraphs carefully, requires rethinking and rewriting, and pushes students to sharpen their reasoning and write what they mean. That is, it works when the teacher is skilled, motivated and blessed with enough time to do what needs to be done. As always, there ain't no free lunch.

In what I think of as an earlier version of assigned TV-viewing, I used the lyrics of popular rock songs as a way of teaching poetry to my high school juniors, who, in the days of ability grouping 1-5, were "4's." This was 1965, when the Beach Boys were singing "Fun, Fun, Fun."

> Well, she's got her daddy's car; she can cruise to the hamburger stand now;
> She forgot about the library like she told her old man now;
> With the radio blasting she's cruising just as fast as she can now,
> And she'll have fun, fun, fun til her daddy takes the T-Bird away.

I assigned it. We played the 45 record in class. Some students transcribed the lyrics. Everyone had to write a short summary of the story (leading to the observation that poems may tell stories). We discussed how the "poet" produced rhyme. As a group, we figured out where the stresses were and what would happen if we moved some words around. All but the last verse end with the same line, or a variant, and that led to further discussion of poetic strategy. Before long that class was reading and analyzing "Dulce et Decorum Est," Wilfred Owen's powerful anti-war poem, and Edna St. Vincent Millay's "Renascence."

The same techniques work today, as talented teachers prove every week. Students assigned to watch and analyze "The Cosby Show," "thirtysomething" and other series can easily transfer those skills and interest to *To Kill a Mockingbird* and *Our Town*.

"Media literacy" courses raise an important question about means and ends. The expressed goal of some of these courses is to teach students to "read" television, that is, to understand the differences among news reports, commercials, documentaries, editorials and other programs. A teacher in Norman, Oklahoma, told *The New York Times*:

> In this course kids become aware that they are consumers of television, which they've been all their lives. It's supposed to make them less susceptible to manipulation by the media, because they know what's going on.

Other "media literacy" courses involve actual production and broadcast over cable. Fairfax, Virginia, has state-of-the-art production facilities in its high school, and student-produced programs are carried on a public access channel there. In some courses, students write and produce news programs, game shows, even soap operas.

According to the *Times*, a high school in Oakland, California, is using a media course to keep potential dropouts in school. The course combines vocational training in journalism with classes that use the media to teach basic skills. To that end, students write and videotape their own commercials to help with their own writing and speaking.

Unfortunately, however, their principal teacher (and role model?) speaks this way: "Having to sell something is a real good way to develop verbal skills. They have to be real specific about the language they use."

Back to means and ends: In my view, media literacy courses designed to move students toward clearly defined academic goals make sense. Teaching children that "they are consumers of television" should take about 10 minutes, and one hardly needs a course for that. As for making children "less susceptible to manipulation," the other goal described by the teacher in Norman, that is a worthy aim. But getting there requires that students understand logic, rhetoric and propaganda. If teachers can use television as the entry point, as a hook, to teaching about these subjects, that's well and good. But, again, television is a means, not an end.

Another form of assigned viewing is the infamous Channel One, the Whittle Communications venture. Channel One, as most everybody knows by now, is a 12-minute daily newscast, of which two minutes are commercials. Schools receive video equipment worth thousands of dollars in return for making students watch the daily newscast and commercials. And while the deal-making has been banned in California, New York and Rhode Island, Whittle Communications says it has persuaded more than 5,500 schools in 45 states to accept the equipment and show its program.

When Whittle Communications announced its plan and began a pilot test, educators argued endlessly about the propriety of forcing kids to watch commercials. Whittle's opponents proclaimed, sanctimoniously, that "our children are not for sale," conveniently overlooking the numerous inroads that cereal companies, milk producers, makers of feminine hygiene products and scads of other corporations made into our schools long ago, with the approval of the educators. (Whittle, a brilliant salesman, got into schools years earlier with "free" billboards that featured an uplifting message [e.g., "stay in school"] ringed with commercial messages.)

The Whittle argument, no less pious, was in two parts. Step one: No children should be deprived of access to modern communication just because a school board is too poor or too backward, so we will provide equal opportunity for all children. Step two: Our children think that Chernobyl is Cher's real first name, and our newscast will end that appalling ignorance, thus helping make America No. 1 again. Equal opportunity, Education and the Flag!

In 1990 I debated Mr. Whittle in front of an audience of about 150 teachers and principals. My objection, incidentally, was not to the commercials but to the passive nature of the enterprise — more sitting there and being talked at. During the hour-long debate, perhaps 15 educators spoke up, and the majority expressed no qualms about the commercials. Rather, they wanted the "free" equipment.

However, the teacher I recall most clearly from that morning was a woman from Florida who taught in a school with Channel One already installed. She didn't particularly like the interruption or the required viewing, she said, but she had built a course around it. Her students were studying "persuasion," using Whittle's commercials as cases in point. They were learning about argument, propaganda and logic, and they were trying their hand at writing persuasive essays. Mr. Whittle and I both applauded her initiative and her pedagogy.

The single best use of television in schools is the hands-on approach. When children get to make their own television, great things happen from a number of vantage points. First, it's active learning, which is the best and most effective type. Second, it's cooperative learning, because no one can make good television alone. (Schools, parenthetically, are perhaps the only institution that penalize you for cooperation. In the real world, it makes sense to ask for help if you're stuck. In school, that's called cheating.) Making television also teaches the important skills of writing clearly and accurately. At the same time, it encourages creativity (in shots, angles, lighting, presentation, etc.).

And there's an added benefit: Students who spend time making television are empowered. They begin to understand the medium and thus gain power over it. No longer will they be "qualified" to become couch potatoes, because those who work at making good television quickly lose their willingness to tolerate a steady diet of mediocrity.

Making television is not expensive. A camcorder, two playback machines and a simple editing board can be purchased for less than $3,000.

Buying in quantity would further reduce the costs. Even in these tight times, a savvy school principal ought to be able to wheel and deal for a couple of complete sets of equipment.

A related and ultimately more powerful and effective use of video technology is known as "multi-media," in which video is just one medium among several. Strictly speaking, it's not television, although a camcorder is basic equipment.

The computer is the core of multi-media. It runs a powerful program like *Hypercard* (Macintosh) or *Linkways* (IBM) that enables groups of students to produce their own multi-media projects.

Imagine, for example, a report on the Great Pyramids. Pictures of the pyramids would be videotaped but fed directly into the computer in a process called "digitizing." Other material could be captured from a videodisc encyclopedia, again fed directly into the computer. The student would read the report's written material, and music could be added using a compact disc. The final project could be transferred to a videotape or kept on the computer disc. On disc it remains interactive; that is, the reader can skip to any part of the report by touching a particular part of the screen.

I've seen third-graders working together competently to create their own reports on "The Great Wall of China" and "Armadillos." In one wonderful classroom in East Lansing, Michigan, I watched two groups of four students work on their multi-media projects while other groups of students worked at their desks on math. The teacher moved from group to group, as needed. And when she turned her back, no one was distracted. Multi-media (and cooperative learning) were allowing her to be "the guide on the side," instead of the usual teacher role of "sage on the stage."

At Cincinnati Country Day School, multi-media has allowed students to take off, to go far beyond requirements and assignments. Just as making television empowers learners, so too does multi-media invite exploration and intellectual rigor.

Clearly multiple media are involved: camcorder, computer, VCR, CD player and laserdisc player. It's not television, but it's the most exciting use of technology I've witnessed in 16 years of reporting about schools.*

---

* The best sources of information about multi-media that I know are Fred D'Ignazio and Sharon Goth-Tew, Teacher Explorer Center, 509 Burcham, East Lansing, Michigan 48823; and Joe Hofmeister and Joyce Rudowski, Cincinnati Country Day School, 6905 Given Road, Cincinnati, Ohio 45243.

Is it expensive? Well, it certainly can be, if you want to buy everything new and top-of-the-line. But if you're willing to be a scavenger, then you might spend exactly nothing to get started.

Leaving school aside, is television the most powerful educational tool ever invented? Yes it is, but, outside of school, it is used to sell, to persuade, to amuse. "Educational television" is not an oxymoron, but neither is it an irresistible force in our society.

Let me confess: I believe in educational television and have worked in and around the neighborhood since 1983. Eight years ago I helped spend nearly $2 million on a public television series, "Your Children, Our Children," that was designed to educate the American public about child-rearing and to improve the lives of children. In one program, viewers watched a baby die, despite the heroic efforts of doctors and nurses, and they learned that most infant deaths were preventable. We showed how society could save millions of dollars, as well as lives, by providing low-cost prenatal care. That was broadcast in 1984, and today the country's infant death figures are virtually unchanged. This national disgrace continues, despite our highly-acclaimed "educational" broadcast.

Another program in our series was about child neglect and abuse. I daresay that most people think of horrific beatings and scaldings when they hear the phrase "child abuse." But, as we showed, verbal abuse and physical and emotional neglect are far more prevalent — but equally likely to leave permanent scars. As we had done in our report on infant death, we highlighted low-cost, effective and non-intrusive ways of helping parents. Sad to say, the statistics on abuse and neglect are just as disturbing today as they were when our program was broadcast.

I could go on. Each program in the seven-part series brought a problem to life and provided examples of workable solutions. We went further; we provided, free of charge, attractive, solution-oriented pamphlets in English and Spanish. We worked with community groups to publicize the series, and the solutions.

Our goal was to change the world. Now, I am certain that we helped some parents and some children, and Robert Browning's directive that "man's aim should exceed his grasp" is some comfort, but the fact remains that the world did not change, that American social attitudes toward children are not much different in 1991 than they were in 1984.

Despite that expensive and time-consuming lesson, I continue to believe that television has unmatched power to educate citizens and change society. It can expose ineptitude and wrongdoing, and it can illuminate success. To vary the old phrase, it can show the water to the world, but it can't lead anyone there, let alone make you drink.

But as for educators, *please* stop using television as a whipping boy to explain your failure to provide a coherent, academically demanding curriculum for our children. Television itself belongs in schools, not as an end in itself, but as a means to mastery of essential skills.

John Merrow is host of "Learning Matters" on The Learning Channel, and from 1985 to 1990 was education correspondent for "The MacNeil/Lehrer NewsHour."

6

Pay No Attention to That Man Behind the Curtain

Charles T. Salmon

Amy, a fourth-grader, shifts uncomfortably in her seat and chews on her pencil's eraser as she re-reads the clue for 4-down in the "Collective Bargaining Crossword Puzzle": "What is the term for a disagreement that workers may have with management?"

"It's not *negotiations* or *collective bargaining*," she muses, "I remember that much." Finally, after counting the number of letters — nine — and eliminating words that are either too long or short, she announces, "Grievance. That's it, grievance." With a satisfied grin, she pencils in the letters and proudly folds her hands on her desk, thereby signaling to her teacher that she is finished with her assignment.

As the bell rings to announce recess, the teacher collects the crosswords from the children and announces, "Tomorrow we'll continue learning about the role of unions in society as we study the difference between strikes and boycotts. I'll show you a video called 'The Wrath of Grapes,' and then you can write a story about why somebody should or shouldn't boycott grapes."

By this point the children are barely listening. They burst into the hallways and then out of the exits to the playground. In their haste and enthusiasm to escape the classroom, they don't stop to think of where the day's lesson plan came from, who designed the crossword puzzle, or why it is important for fourth-graders to learn the distinction between strikes and boycotts. After all, children are in school to learn the material presented, not to question the selection of a discussion topic or the source of a teacher's information.

As it turns out, the lessons on collective bargaining and strikes and boycotts were the product of a seminar for elementary school teachers sponsored by the International Brotherhood of Teamsters in 1987. The video was produced by the United Farm Workers and made available to educators free of charge. As innovative as the pedagogical combination of videos and crossword puzzles for 9-year-olds may seem, the involvement of an interest group in the design of curriculum materials is anything but unique. In fact, the lessons described above represent only two of literally thousands of lessons developed by corporations, governments and interest groups for use in elementary and high school classrooms. These efforts are essentially components of broader communication campaigns, designed and managed by public relations and advertising professionals to influence the thoughts, attitudes and behaviors of future generations of commercial and political consumers.

In the most comprehensive work on this topic to date, *Hucksters in the Classroom* (Center for Study of Responsive Law, 1979), author Sheila Harty documents the long history of these campaigns. More than 60 years ago, for example, a major manufacturer of consumer goods offered free bars of soap and illustrated booklets on the history of soap-making to teachers and school systems. As early as 1934, Educators Progress Service published a guide to free materials intended "to aid teachers with the high turnover of information on current affairs and to offer industry a chance to participate in the exchange."

Concern among school administrators about the use of these materials has an almost equally long history. Harty found that a 1929 "Report of the Committee on Propaganda in the Schools" ominously warned that "We have hundreds of outside agencies each striving to exploit the school in the interest of its particular commodity or idea. Their resources are large and their methods of penetration ingenious." Included in the report, Harty adds, was a list of 82 commercial items found in a single New England city classroom.

Concerns such as these have not abated over the years. Organizations such as the National Education Association and the American Association of School Administrators periodically have issued advisory reports on the topic. In 1955, for example, the latter organization issued a guide entitled "Beware of Too Much Help" that warned educators of the self-serving interests of organizations offering "free" and convenient curriculum materials to schools. Despite the occasional warnings and calls for reform, the controversy remains unresolved; later this year the National Association of Partners in Education is expected to issue a new set of recommendations for the regulation of corporate marketing in schools.

The origins and goals of the vast majority of such influence attempts go unnoticed and unquestioned by the general public. In fact it is probably safe to say that most parents are unaware of the full extent to which social and commercial marketers have successfully gained access to their children's classrooms. Only when the influence attempts are obvious, as when advertisers publicly bicker over the opportunity to sponsor an athletic scoreboard or when religious and secular groups heatedly debate the teaching of creationism versus evolution, do parents and policy-makers become sufficiently outraged to fight what they consider to be propagandistic intrusion into the pristine environments of their schools.

But such objections tend to be relatively rare because the vast majority of school-based influence campaigns are covert rather than overt. Because parents and policy-makers are unaware of most persuasive efforts and protest only the blatant ones, they effectively penalize those organizations that are aboveboard in their attempts to manipulate and paradoxically reward those that are more sly.

But while these campaign efforts may go unnoticed by parents, the same cannot be said for teachers. Why are these covert persuasion campaigns so successful with educators? In a nutshell, economics.

By some estimates, the average school spends less than five percent of its budget on curriculum materials, with the vast remainder allocated to staff salaries and utilities. As school budgets suffer directly and indirectly from ailing state and federal economies, administrators are under increasing pressure to make more severe cuts in their budgets, and curriculum allotments often are among the first items to go. Simultaneously, teachers, saddled with a myriad of responsibilities and arguably undercompensated for their efforts, are expected to keep informed about a rapidly changing environment while effectively discharging their regular duties. Not surprisingly, the availability of neatly packaged curriculum materials, sometimes including sophisticated videos, graphics, charts, transparencies, pamphlets, product samples, comic books and even offers of guest speakers, seems a godsend.

These classroom materials are thus prime examples of what communications researcher Oscar Gandy terms "information subsidies," i.e., information made available to a needy consuming organization at an attractive price. In the generic information-exchange process, a consuming organization seeks and acquires information to the extent that its value is high relative to its cost, while the producing organization distributes the information to the extent that its expected return, usually in the form of influence over others, similarly is high relative to its cost.

In the specific case of school-based campaigns, the cost to the consuming organization usually is little or nothing; most materials are free. Even when the information subsidy requires the use of expensive technology, the cost to the consumer is often rendered negligible by the producer. Whittle Communications, for example, has offered schools thousands of dollars worth of free television sets, video equipment and satellite dishes in return for their showing its Channel One news program and advertising to students. In an era of underfinanced schools and overworked teachers and administrators, such an offer can be too attractive to pass up.

As is the case for most exchange processes, this one is characterized by a high degree of symmetry. Corporations, special interest groups and governments generally are not engaging in purely charitable, asymmetric exchanges through their proffering of subsidized materials; they are making calculated investments and expecting reasonable returns. In a few cases the investments are made to achieve short-term objectives and the resulting payoffs are immediate and tangible. Far more often, however, the investments are long-term and the payoffs both delayed and often intangible. In general, these payoffs involve the formation of favorable attitudes or habitual behaviors pertaining to specific products, organizations or lifestyles.

The school is an ideal environment for forging enduring attitudes and behaviors. Schoolchildren are a captive audience, conveniently assembled together at regular time intervals in the same known setting. More malleable than most adults, children are also less likely to question or dispute "facts," whatever they may be.

Numerous corporations, large and small, have capitalized on these near-idyllic conditions for influence. For example, a recent report in the *San Antonio Business Journal* described a campaign by a local credit union to encourage elementary school students — from kindergarten to eighth grade — to deposit their spare change in its savings accounts. According to the credit union's general manager, the savings program initially was an offshoot of classes on credit and banking that the institution had offered to seventh- and eighth-graders. To date, 500 student accounts have been opened; more importantly, the students' parents are eligible members of the credit union, creating the potential for an even greater future supply of depositors and borrowers.

Similar behavioral goals have been sought by the major computer manufacturers. Companies in the computer industry have donated millions of dollars worth of equipment and software to educational facilities of all types and at all levels. This equipment has, without doubt, enabled thousands of children and adolescents to develop much greater computer sophistication than would otherwise have been possible in the absence of the companies' philanthropy. However the benefits to the corporations exceed the mere satisfaction of altruism; by training children with their — rather than their competitor's —equipment and operating systems, computer manufacturers may have ingrained long-term brand loyalty among generations of prospective computer hackers.

Media corporations have taken a similar approach in attempting to market their products to teachers and school systems. *Time, Newsweek, The New York Times* and *The New Yorker* all offer special incentives to teachers and students in efforts to cultivate loyal followings among young consumers. To briefly digress, what is particularly interesting about the marketing of these products is the double standard pertaining to the control of print- versus broadcast-media products. That is, few if any school administrators would even pause to reflect on the propriety of allowing the publications listed above to aggressively market their products for classroom use, nor would they be likely to question the use of those publications in class assignments and discussions. At the same time, all of those publications contain as much or more advertising content as does their highly criticized broadcast counterpart, Channel One. This suggests that it is the power of the broadcast media in general, rather than opposition to commercialism *per se*, which may be fueling criticisms of the use of commercial broadcast systems in schools.

Other corporations have developed innovative contests and games as mechanisms for gaining entry into schools. For example:

- a major manufacturer of a shoe deodorizer sponsored a "Rotten Sneaker Contest" for students at schools throughout the country.
- Both Levi Strauss and Lands End have organized campaigns within campaigns, i.e., campaigns targeted at communications professors to encourage

their students to compete by — what else? — designing promotional campaigns for the companies' clothing.

One of the most established genres of school-based publicity campaigns is public health. These campaigns often are conducted with the assistance of local or state public health officials or other health-related organizations. For example, the Penn State Nutrition Center has developed a game show entitled "Alcohol: Are You in Jeopardy?" for use by teachers in junior and senior high schools, and the American School Health Association has designed a series of experiments with which teachers can demonstrate the deleterious effects of cigarette smoke on plants.

The prevalence of school-based health programs is made apparent by a recent news release from the National Association of Elementary School Principals that describes the results of a nationwide survey of its membership. According to the survey, 88 percent of the responding principals report offering drug education programs to children before the fourth grade, with 58 percent beginning in kindergarten. Although fewer principals, 63 percent, report offering AIDS awareness programs in elementary schools, a full 23 percent of these start in kindergarten as well.

Health-behavior campaigns are not sponsored solely by public health agencies, but are offered by a number of corporations as well. According to Sheila Harty, such programs over the years have included:

- McDonald's "Nutrition Action Pack," designed to "introduce new foods and nutrition concepts at an early age when new tastes and ideas are more readily accepted. . . . ";

- "Mr. Peanut's Guide to Physical Fitness";

- General Mills' "Education Catalog," describing films, filmstrips, books and other classroom materials available to educators;

- the National Soft Drink Association's booklet entitled "The Story of Soft Drinks";

- Kraft's "Guide to Cheese Nutrition"; and

- the Manufacturing Chemists Association's booklet entitled "Food Additives: Who Needs Them?"

What are the social implications of these types of persuasion campaigns? Foremost is their potential for both expanding and limiting the ability of schools to provide a curriculum of breadth and depth. On one hand, the possibility exists that these externally funded campaigns allow a particularly resource-poor school to expand its capacity for serving the public interest. With the information subsidy, the school may be able to educate its students about some important topic in health or politics that it otherwise would be incapable of addressing. The provision of free computers and communications hardware may greatly expand the school's capability to train students for meaningful careers rather than dead-end jobs. Acceptance of a corporation's plan to raise funds for the school (and simultaneously promote the company's image) may allow the school to survive in the face of otherwise fatal budgetary cuts.

On the other hand, the possibility exists that these campaigns may actually inhibit diversity and innovation. This is because the organizations most likely to be in a position to sponsor such subsidies — and to be welcomed into classrooms by educational gatekeepers — are those already benefiting from the status quo and in possession of substantial financial power and legitimacy. Because there is no pretense that these campaigns are balanced or exhaustive in the sense of giving equally strong endorsement of all issue positions, certain views, attitudes and behaviors consistently will be promoted to the exclusion of others. Influence campaigns conducted in U.S. schools and focusing on the topic of economics, for example, are likely to promote the merits of capitalism and free enterprise rather than to train students to evaluate the relative strengths and weaknesses of alternative political and economic systems.

In other words, the primary function of most school-based campaigns probably is to reinforce existing customs, systems and norms and in the process establish boundaries on children's creativity and innovation, rather than to hone critical acumen. This conclusion is similar to that of French philosopher Pierre Bordieu in his description of how educational systems reproduce the cultural and social values of the societies in which they operate. To Bordieu, the educational system "is in fact one of the most effective means of perpetuating the existing social pattern."

The means of this reproduction, as we have seen, can be blatant or subtle, but they can also be implicit as well as explicit. For example, psychologist Eliott Aronson notes that basic arithmetic problems assigned in U.S. schools tend to deal with such topics as "buying, selling, renting, working for wages and computing interest," thereby contributing to the transmission of the dominant cultural values of American society. It is unlikely that widespread use of these arithmetic problems reflects the outcome of some massive, coordinated influence campaign. More likely, it merely reflects the extent to which teachers are products of their culture and its terminology.

The power of educational systems to instill cultural values and beliefs was demonstrated recently by an incident following the Gulf War. Confronted with seemingly insurmountable evidence that its troops had been badly routed and its annexation of Kuwait thwarted, Iraqi leaders remained surprisingly unruffled in the days immediately following the cease-fire. Indeed, Saddam Hussein went so far as to boldly declare that his forces had been victorious in confronting the forces of Satan, a conclusion that initially elicited anger, then bafflement and finally ridicule from American leaders who had expected a more contrite demeanor on the part of so thoroughly a defeated foe. However the reasoning behind the Iraqi leader's composure was soon made apparent in a statement in *Al-Thawra*, the newspaper of the ruling Baath Party: "Victory is not how many tanks or planes we or the enemy used. . . . Victory is the face that you acquire in the history books."

In other words, control of history books — i.e., the education and socialization of youth — translates into control of facts, meanings, interpretations and values for future generations. It is the power to redefine the terrorist as patriot, the vanquished as victor, and the manipulator as benefactor. The important question for policymakers and the public is not *whether* values and special interests are represented in classrooms, but rather *whose* values and interests are represented, and whose excluded.

Charles T. Salmon is associate professor of mass communication at the University of Wisconsin at Madison.

7

Hollywood High

Patricia Aufderheide

Through a funhouse mirror, '80s movies set in high school reflected disturbing social realities — about the power of commercial youth culture, about authority, about the powerful dividers of class and race. And they could make you feel downright sorry for the teacher.

Of course, it's only a movie. The troubling part comes when you realize that movies draw, if not on reality, on widespread perceptions of reality in order to sell. It gets worse when you realize that sometimes not only the kids but our nation's educational leaders seem to be more in synch with Hollywood than with the problems of their own local schools.

In the late '70s and early '80s a subgenre bloomed, the comedy or drama set in a middle-class high school. Kidpix, as they're known in the trade, are a product of marketing demographics — big ones. Teens spent an estimated $79 billion in 1990 — about the size of the Argentine national economy.

Soon after *American Graffiti* became a monster hit in 1973, the handwriting was on the wall, or on the concession stand: The money was in the 12-24 crowd, especially the teens, who go to the same movie repeatedly and who have unprecedented spending power. Then National Lampoon's *Animal House* hit the kid jackpot in 1978. Kidpix — movies like *Fast Times at Ridgemont High* (1982), *Risky Business* (1983), *The Breakfast Club* (1985), among so many others that their titles and images blur in the mind — raked in dollars for the entertainment industry during the '80s. Of course, the not-yet-married have always been the staple audience of theatrical movies, but before youth culture, when young people were still second-class citizens in the marketplace, they wanted to see movies about adults.

It only makes good marketing sense that kidpix put the focus on the kids. And not just on them, but on the separate and lucrative commercial culture they're immersed in — from bedroom hideaways with beamed-in music video to their jobs and social life at the shopping mall. Education often isn't even in the picture; it's the irritant, the pointless information that clogs up a perfectly good weekend, hallway romance or impish adventure.

What may raise an eyebrow is that in kidpix, usually set in a perpetually sunny, generic middle-class America, social conflict is a driving element. That might seem surprising, not only in a society where most poll respondents identify themselves as middle-class but in an industry where the cardinal rule still is, "If you want to send a message, call Western Union." But it makes sense if you're looking to propel a drama enclosed by the world of middle-class high schoolers.

The American high school has been celebrated as "the last classless society," the last social moment in most American lives when people of different social tiers mix. To some degree, given residential patterns and segregation, that's always been a fiction. But it's true that high school — the institution that serves that demographic creation of industrial society, adolescence — is a society unto itself, and that its world is as much about socialization as it is about formal education. And it's more class-ful than classless. As John Sayles' *Baby, It's You* (1983), a cross-class high school love affair set in the '60s, showcased, the social tensions of the wider society are enacted there more intensely than people have to experience them at any other time in their lives.

But in the pre-youth-culture era, teachers along with parents and parents' associations acted vigorously as a governor on the furnace of social conflict. They had a crucial advantage: the students' own aspiration to be adults. They were, willy nilly, role models as well as enforcers.

Eighties kidpix handily abolished this element. At their bubbliest, they not only put the kids in the center of their stories but made authorities the butt of the joke, often not even giving them the dignity of a weighty villain. At their darkest, movies like *River's Edge* (1986) and *Suburbia* (1983, also known as *The Wild Side*) bleakly showcased middle-class adolescent nihilism, predicated on a despair about adults and adulthood generally. (*River's Edge*, drawn from a real-life murder incident, appealed more to critics than to teenagers, though; and the independently made *Suburbia* sank into a distribution black hole.) Either way, they sold the image of a hermetically autonomous adolescence.

In these films students wage their social battles on their own with the weapons of consumer culture: fashion, celebrity, attitude. (Not often drugs, though — in the Hollywoodized middle-class high school, that's the big unmentionable.) Attitude is that endlessly transmutable feature of teen identity, to which all the commercial accoutrements contribute.

The kids, not the teachers, are in charge of their own education. As the heroine (Winona Ryder) of the black comedy *Heathers* — one-stop shopping for teen-film stereotypes, and a punchy satire of the subgenre — says of the most viciously popular girl in school: "Heather says she teaches people how to live." The teachers, by contrast, function as convenient enemies and buffoons, icons of the bleak promise of adult-hood and the separate reality of youth culture.

Classroom learning is patently irrelevant. New Deal policies, the Russian revolution, the Platt Amendment, frog dissection — it's all just dropped in to signal that stuff we have to get right for the test but that has no relevance to our lives. (Quick, what *was* the Platt Amendment?) And it's not even a question of making it relevant. Let the eponymous hero of *Ferris Bueller's Day Off* (1986) explain it, as he faces the prospect of studying about European socialism: "I don't plan on being European. They could be fascists or anarchists, that wouldn't change the fact that I don't have a car."

Good thing Ferris didn't go on *Bill and Ted's Excellent Adventure* (1989) — although, come to think of it, it might not have made much difference in his attitude. In that helium-weight comedy, a garage-band duo are plunged, by a character from the future, into the past, European and elsewhere, so they can pass their history oral report. They capture Socrates, Genghis Khan and Lincoln among others, who are dazzled by mall culture and finally boogie for the student assembly. In a music-video-like performance, Lincoln delivers a parody of the Gettysburg Address, with the rousing finale: "Let's party, dudes!" Indeed, not only the present but the future belongs to the lunkish Bill and Ted — their guardian has rescued them from imminent separation (Ted's policeman father wants to send him to military school if he doesn't pass history class) because in the future the entire society is built around worship of Bill and Ted's heavy metal band.

If learning is irrelevant, so are the teachers, universally nerds, jerks or tyrants. Authority is the traditional butt of American movie comedy, of course, but authority is funny in Kidpix because it's vacuous. When authority is the enemy, it's because it's petty, arbitrary, irrelevant to the passions and issues of the kids. Even the tyrants are only tyrants up to the parking lot (and their cars aren't nearly as nice as those of the students). The occasional good adult authority, like the mad scientist of *Back to the Future* (1985), is a non-establishment figure, an idiosyncratic fringe element who resonates to the kids' self-perception.

The teachers are mere obstacles — some more amusing buffoons than others — to the real business of life. They certainly have no relation to the students other than prison-guard or torturer. Take the history teacher of *Fast Times at Ridgemont High*, who shows up in the poster-decorated bedroom — which looks strangely like one of the MTV video-jockey sets — of the gonzo surfer on the night of the big dance, solely in order to grill him on the American revolution and thus take his revenge for the surfer's insolence. (Only a movie made from a teen perspective would show a teacher wasting his own weekend evening to grill a sloucher.) In *The Breakfast Club*, a cruelly authoritarian teacher — he's forgotten how to be a kid — interns the students with sneering contempt and then, a failed but resigned '60s idealist, grouses to the janitor about how the kids are "worse" every year. And in *Back to the Future*, the teacher's only role is to shred the self-esteem of the hero (Michael J. Fox). "You've got a real attitude problem," he says, adding that the boy's father did too. "No McFly ever amounted to anything in Hill Valley."

The teachers who try to get on the kids' wavelengths make the best butts of jokes. Take the "touchy-feely" ex-hippie of the black comedy *Heathers* — a self-professed '60s idealist whom even the other teachers scorn. (The near past is the most passionately rejected.) Faced with mounting apparent suicides in the school, she asks her students to join her to "connect this cafeteria into one mighty circuit." She's also alerted the media, of course, and exhorts the students: "On TV, let's show them how you *feel!*" The students mount a spectacle the irony of which bypasses the teacher, caught up in her own narcissistic dreaminess.

Ineffectual authority at school — Ferris Bueller's dean of students rails about his capacity to "govern this student body," making gaffe after gaffe — is echoed at home. But these parents aren't misguided authorities who need to wake up, like the parents of the 1955 *Rebel without a Cause*.

Sometimes they're simply thugs, insensitively barking orders and criticism. Sometimes they're self-indulgent and neglectful. And sometimes they're patronized innocents, hapless dependents of their own children — or simply, pleasantly, absent. In any case, the old adolescent complaint, "They don't understand me," becomes, in these movies, "They'd never understand us." Even in *The Breakfast Club*, where parents and teachers are responsible for the kids' misery — one kid says he stirred up trouble "for my old man; I wanted him to think I was cool," and another, asked why her parents are so bad, says in a whisper, "They ignore me" — the kids reject the teacher's command to write an essay on the theme "Who am I?" They ask, "Why do you care?" without expecting an answer, instead finding self-realization in a spontaneous group therapy session.

The kids, who shop or work (or both) at the mall, struggle toward a sense of self in relation to each other and the challenge of the go-go '80s: making it. In the works of John Hughes, who either wrote or directed the major hits of this mini-genre (*16 Candles* [1984], *Pretty in Pink* [1986], *The Breakfast Club*, *Some Kind of Wonderful* [1987]), that means climbing the social ladder one's peers have erected without losing your integrity. Hughes' '80s films (he recently directed *Home Alone*) usually featured some kind of hermetic class conflict in which the heroes are the hard-working, misunderstood, poor kids, often in love with someone from the disparaged wealthy crowd. From locker room to high school hallway to the mall and back to the high school dance, the romance is pursued to a happy ending, when common decency is rediscovered and the myth of the universal middle class reaffirmed.

Success is sometimes romantic resolution, sometimes prestige, sometimes business, and sometimes all of these at once. The hero (played by Tom Cruise) of *Risky Business* overexemplifies the '80s when he manages to mount a successful prostitution ring out of his parents' upper-middle-class home, and even draws the Princeton recruiter into it. Other kids aspire to solvency, through hard work at the mall burger shop. Ferris Bueller's a hero because he's a consummate con man. At the end of *Back to the Future* the hero achieves the ultimate success: He redesigns not only his life but his entire family's by altering the past, gaining upscale professional parents *and* a cool car of his own.

But it's hard work being cool, and they know it. The heroine of *Heathers* explains to the young psychopath who asks her why she hangs around with girls she doesn't like, "They're people I work with, and our job is being popular and shit." And the ultimate self-dramatizing melodrama — suicide — is always an option.

No wonder the teachers don't count. What do they know about popularity or '80s star Pat Benatar? What's the Platt Amendment compared to an abortion, suicide — or being without a car? Gone in these movies is the angst of *Rebel without a Cause*, where the James Dean character longed for proper patriarchy. These kids are playing on their own, for real, and for cash.

The kidpix explosion created a galaxy of new young stars, most of them (Molly Ringwald, Ally Sheedy and Winona Ryder apart) male: Tom Cruise, Michael J. Fox, Sean Penn, Matthew Broderick and Emilio Estevez, among others. These actors' stars rose with the popularity of the images they projected. The male characters, either bright screw-ups or cheerful dim bulbs, were droll wiseacres, seemingly juvenile but in reality new leaders of an insouciant youth culture. Their great achievement is one of performance, a bold, daring self-presentation. (It's interesting that the one high school film of this era that was interracial and cross-class, *Fame* [1979], was about a school of performing arts. There teachers *could* exercise authority because they were a gateway to a life of performance.) Girls in these films win autonomy only in two gender-segregated arenas: fashion (among girls) and feeling (with the boys). The image of the white, middle-class teen world in these movies may be divorced from that of adults, but some things, like gender roles, don't change.

With the more sober and recessionary '90s, as well as with a shrinking teenage population, the gas has gone out of kidpix. They spoke as much to the bubble of false prosperity generally as they did to the power of the middle-class teen marketplace. These days, the wryly anti-ideal nuclear family — think of *Married . . . with Children, The Simpsons* and *Roseanne* on TV — is setting a new trend. Kidpix also echoed, in teen terms, a pervasive '80s disillusionment among American consumers with authority — seen elsewhere, for instance, in the rash of films about Vietnam and its aftermath. There, the grunt became the hero precisely because he was the put-upon victim of callous authority, the wielder of responsibility without power. With the Gulf war, a parody of the Gettysburg address may no longer seem so funny.

They also took populist, often self-contradictory myths of middle-class mobility — anyone can make it; being rich is bad but getting rich is great; the past is prologue; do it yourself; thumb your nose at authority and also get in charge; look for the individual solution to social problems — and put them to work with the malled confines of commercial youth culture. Maybe it's that rather lumpy collection of myths that then-Secretary of Education William Bennett responded to when, at the height of college student demonstrations for institutional disinvestment in South Africa-related stocks, he advised prospective college students rather to consider "disinvestment" in their stereo systems and spring vacations. And maybe it's that collection of myths that made it possible for Hollywood to trust — with good evidence at the box office — that films about the white middle-class would appeal across racial and class lines among youthful audiences.

Eighties movies about high school life at the upper and lower ends of the social spectrum more directly commented on the roiling tensions over education and its social function. What's scary is how well they echoed Reagan-era rhetoric about the educational crisis among America's disadvantaged.

These movies — at the upper end of the scale, *Dead Poets Society* (1989), and at the lower end, *Stand and Deliver* (1987) and *Lean on Me* (1989) — were not pitched to the teen market but to adults. They not only took place within school but were about school, and even about the classroom. In those movies teachers were important, even life-saving role models.

Of course, the goals of education are entirely different for the different classes. For the rich and white it's about self-fulfillment, self-expression, stimulating the life of the imagination. For the poor and people of color, it's about discipline.

In the prep school of *Dead Poets Society* — set in a hazily post-World War II past — the putative protagonist is the boy who will eventually commit suicide, plagued by his rigid father's elite aspirations for him. But his central problem, as that of the film, is that of authority properly wielded, and that puts the teacher at the crux of the drama.

This is not a high school with teeming hallways. It's a small school, rich in tradition (the boys see pictures of their fathers on the wall). The boys are cowed by the combined authority of rigid masters and demanding parents, until Mr. Keating comes along. As played by Robin Williams, he's a sprite, but a sprite with bite. When he tells his students to tear out the pedantic introduction to their poetry books, by God they do it. When he tells them to jump up on his desk, they hop up there. When he commands them to have imagination, they produce it.

Mr. Keating's command to imaginative liberation takes place in the same intellectual universe that William Bennett so touted, first at the National Endowment for the Humanities and then at the Department of Education: in the safely splendid world of stamped-and-approved dead white male writers. No danger of ugly questions of multiculturalism or Afrocentric curricula here. These kids, ensconced not only in an all-white, all-male prep school but in the pre-computer, pre-drugs era, rebel (on order by Keating, of course) by studying the Romantics and not the Realists. It's a timid example of Bennett's generous claim that the five-foot-shelf could be expanded a foot or two if necessary. Although Keating presumably heralds the same imaginative wave that brought us the beatniks (and one of the kids wears a token beret), there's not a hint of the brewing cultural upset. And so *Dead Poets Society* offers a two-hour return to a spurious past in which the educational questions boil down to more or less conformity within unquestioned confines.

Bennett also loved the heroes of two films about ghetto school teachers: Jaime Escalante in Los Angeles and Joe Clark in New Jersey. He heralded them, along with other charismatic figures who had a strong disciplinary, pull-yourself-up-by-your-bootstraps message, for producing exemplary schools "that work."

Escalante, a Bolivian immigrant and math teacher in the Los Angeles schools, has gotten students in a low-income, primarily Hispanic school to pass advanced placement calculus tests with strong discipline and motivational methods that include cheerleading and prizes, personal attention to students' home lives, and Saturday sessions. His techniques have drawn fire from colleagues and teachers' unions because they require a much greater workload than normal. Indeed, however charismatic a teacher Escalante is, he's hardly a one-man solution to endemic educational problems among the Hispanic poor, a third of whom drop out before completing high school — the highest dropout rate in the country and one that's growing.

Joe Clark, an African-American teacher, came into a down-at-the-heels New Jersey school plagued with drug and discipline problems and used harsh disciplinary methods, including expelling troublemakers and symbolized by his carrying a baseball bat in the halls. Proudly calling himself a dictator and likening high school to a plantation, he succeeded temporarily in bringing about order and improving test scores (mostly by kicking out the lowest scorers), but at the cost of a sky-high dropout rate and record-breaking teacher turnover.

Betting on a succession of tough-love educational Supermen and Rambos to turn the educational system around may not be much of an educational policy, especially if high schools are run like large factory-prisons, with huge populations and class sizes. But it's great movie material. Hollywood does love a hero. And the minority poor, especially the young, are easy targets for a savior. They can be patronized like the white middle-class kids — subjects of the films pitched to them and their allowances and salaries — could never be.

Stand and Deliver is sensitive to the complexities of the teacher-student relationship while still tubthumping the pull-yourself-up-by-your-bootstraps message. Made partly with public television money for PBS's *American Playhouse* by director Ramon Menendez, it's a low-key ensemble film in which a provoking subdrama is that of the testing board's refusal to accept the high scores — portrayed as a case of institutional racism. Escalante — played by Edward James Olmos, who also had a significant role in the script — is bulwarked by a rich supporting cast, including then-rising stars Lou Diamond Phillips and Andy Garcia. Although we learn little about calculus — the story is about kids coming to realize they can make something of themselves — we do enter into the thick texture of personal relationships Escalante has with the students. Some of the film's heroes are the kids who, despite awesome odds, get a little taste of success.

Lean on Me, directed by the same John Avildsen who gave us *Rocky* (1976) and *The Karate Kid* I and II (1984, 1986), doesn't bother with subtleties. It openly cheerleads for "tough love" policies, and if its hero (played by Morgan Freeman) goes a little overboard, it's all justified in the end. He's pitted not only against drug dealers (with the poor, Hollywood can acknowledge drugs) but the school board and the mayor; he "adopts" a boy and girl student who are set straight. "This is not a damned democracy," he shouts. "We are in a state of emergency and my word is law." The students endorse him: "Mr. Clark believes in us!" "He's like a father!" The film ends with a face-down at the mayor's office between bureaucrats and kids, with Clark triumphant, *Rocky*-like, at the top of the steps.

In *Lean on Me* the hero is Clark, who tramples namby-pamby liberals in his crusade for discipline. And here, discipline *is* education. Leave the quest for self-expression, the small groups, and the intimate and exploratory conversations to the prep school kids. In fact, what was the problem in *Dead Poets Society* is the solution in *Lean on Me*. Of course, neither the problem nor the solution even enters the equation in films pitched to teens themselves.

You expect the movies to thrive on heroes, stereotype and happy endings. So it's not surprising that in '80s high school movies middle-class heroes were the teens themselves; upper class heroes were emotional liberators; and lower-class heroes were law-and-order types. It's not surprising either that the movies should dramatize social tensions that infuse the high school experience. You might even see in '80s teen movies disturbing truths refracted about a collapse of faith in a future that proceeds, in anything but a miraculous way, from the recent past.

But in the end it's only a movie and, in real life high schools, education, equity, and the challenge of authority properly wielded are still at issue. In real life there's no way to go back to the future. There's precious little promise in current Department of Education rhetoric of "choice" — opening up the school system to market forces — to rebalance educational inequities embedded in much larger social ones. Let's hope that '90s educational administrators don't borrow as liberally from the stereotypes purveyed in the movies as '80s educational rhetoric did.

Patricia Aufderheide is an assistant professor in the School of Communication at The American University and a senior editor of *In These Times* newspaper.

8

Amo, Amas . . . Amazing!
Interactive Television Comes of Age

Fred and Victoria Williams

"Caesar duxit magnam legii. . . . "

"Legionem, Dan," prompts Joan Coombs, Cliffside High School Latin teacher. "Accusative case, singular, third declension — takes the '-em' ending."

"Thanks, Mrs. Coombs, shall I go on?"

"Not now," says Coombs, giving Dan her "thank-you" smile. "Let's all take a look at the 1983 National Latin Exam for a few minutes. Martin, you can lead off."

This exchange would not be all that different from an everyday sophomore Latin class (if, indeed, there is such a thing), except that Joan Coombs in her east Bergen County, New Jersey, classroom is about a day's march of the Roman army away from Dan, who sits with his class at Park Ridge High. All this is made possible by one of Bergen County's newest educational innovations, interactive TV classrooms, or "ITV" as the kids call it. The 12 or so students at each site, as well as Joan, can see one another with the help of four TV monitors on two-way video. They can converse naturally through a high-quality, two-way audio system, and, if they want to share a paper, it goes via their fax machines. Students at Park Ridge virtually self-manage their participation in the class, though Principal Charles Montesano sits in should there be any logistical problems (which there are not, so he grades papers from his regular classes).

As you observe ITV classes and talk with students and teachers, you soon sense that while they may be in two physically separated classrooms, they are operating, psychologically speaking, in one electronically created "virtual" classroom. Physical and spatial parameters give way to a kind of intellectual coalescence as students and teacher interact without giving much thought to the telecommunications network that links them. This makes the ITV classroom qualitatively different from the simple use of television in classrooms, as when viewing tapes or receiving over-the-air broadcasts (including via satellite relay). These traditional applications have usually been known as "distance learning."

Most instructional television is distinctively one-way, although some, such as the Texas-based TI-IN service, offer classroom audio feedback via telephone. Satellite-based systems like TI-IN are valuable for bringing educational offerings to remote areas and could be valuable should we ever seriously think about developing a national curriculum. (TI-IN currently has a national program on AIDS in the works.) Eventually we may see the combination of satellite- and network-served classrooms, the former feeding programs into the latter for local distribution and perhaps interaction.

On this winter morning in the ITV classroom, Joan Coombs turns to her Park Ridge students and looks at Martin, who has yet to respond to her request that he begin reading aloud. "Mr. Montesano, you have my permission to throw erasers if we can't wake up a little faster here!" It's 7:30 a.m., a half-hour before the first period of the regular class day. One of the problems of setting up ITV classes is that schools are often on slightly different schedules. Sometimes, as in this case, you solve the problem by offering the class extra early, or during "zero" period as Montesano calls it.

In an era of seemingly endless press coverage of school budget cuts, district takeovers, drugs, crime, and the general failure of the American educational system, there may be a bright spot in the emerging story of interactive television instruction. It is not a panacea — not another generation of educational TV or the whiz-bang (and failed) predictions about uses of computers in the schools. ITV is a transformation as well as an expansion of the instructional environment that offers new opportunities to extend the coverage of talented teachers, to gain economies of scale by sharing resources among schools, and economies of scope by extending the curricula of schools, especially small or rural ones.

Several additional factors also make ITV an interesting innovation to track. For one, most of the development of ITV installations has come from within education, not from outside vendors bearing overextended promises (as with computers, for example). Moreover, one of our largest business sectors — local telephone companies — may increasingly find it in their financial as well as community-service interests to promote ITV because it justifies upgrades of their networks and offers a way around restrictive regulatory barriers. (There are opportunities, too, for cable-TV providers if they can overcome their parochial attitudes.) In all, ITV may be a developing story of considerable public interest.

"Seven in the morning, TVs and fax machines. Is this the future of education?" we ask Park Ridge Superintendent Bob Balentine. We recall stuffy classrooms of some 30 years earlier and feel petrified at the thought of being asked to conjugate *sequesteratus* in the future imperfect tense. "Can you teach Latin better this way?"

"It's Latin this way or not at all," Balentine replies, and we sense this isn't the first time he has answered that question. Today's tight school budgets make it impractical to offer classes that might enroll only 10 or fewer students, and effective Latin teachers — ones who make it their speciality, love the subject, and convey their enthusiasm to their students — are hard to find. Yet there are always students in "college-bound" populations who want Latin, or their parents want them to have it, or they know that Latin will look positive to university admissions or scholarship officers. For them, ITV makes taking the class possible.

"On the other hand," Balentine says, "for all the core subjects like math, English, and even popular foreign languages, we have enough students to justify full-time, on-site teachers and classes. There would be no advantage in having ITV sections. Mainly, ITV opens up new opportunities like teaching Japanese or offering community college courses to outstanding seniors, both of which are being introduced in Bergen County."

Assuming that ITV experiences have been generally positive, we ask Balentine about the negatives: "Are you compromising the instructional process or educational quality by replacing live instruction with ITV?"

"ITV *is* live," he says. "We're too new at this to give you test data, but the students and teachers seem to think our classes are up to par. Our biggest problems are the nitty-grittys of scheduling, getting the necessary coordination among participating schools, and eventually figuring out who will pay whom as we get more into ITV."

At Park Ridge, as in other sites we've visited around the country, students will readily tell you what they like or dislike about ITV. On the positive side they almost always note the break in the routine that an ITV class offers. There is a special kind of comradery that develops among students who have never even met one another, and frequently the mikes and cameras are left on before and after class so as to encourage socializing. Students like their ITV teachers and are astute enough to recognize that those who volunteer for ITV assignments are typically self-confident and effective in the classroom. Currently, most of the ITV teachers, including Joan Coombs, have volunteered to try the system.

On the negative side are many of the same points that Balentine placed among the nitty-grittys of doing ITV. Classes are sometimes scheduled at weird hours, schools have conflicting events (last week Cliffside had finals, Park Ridge did not), and it is difficult to get to the off-campus ITV teacher about the little things — explaining why an assignment wasn't ready, making up a quiz, or getting help with a paper or exam.

One possibly remarkable point — and the students say it is a surprise to them also — is how quickly you adapt to the ITV classroom. As early as the first meeting or two you began to behave as if everybody is in one class. Joan Coombs, who said she froze in front of TV news cameras covering the project, has never had that anxiety with the classroom equipment.

One reason may be that ITV classrooms are really quite simple, not at all the Starship Enterprise that people often expect them to be. About any classroom can be used with a few alterations and additions: replacing traditional desks with chairs and tables; improving the acoustic qualities of ceiling, walls and floors with special coverings; and cutting out any bright window glare. Visible additions are usually four large TV monitors suspended from the ceiling, three to four unobtrusive TV cameras (about the size of an amateur camcorder) that are mounted on the walls or ceiling, equally unobtrusive microphones that lie flat and out of the way on the tables, and, when the room is to serve as a "host," a lectern-based control station for the teacher. Most ITV rooms eventually add a fax machine. Also added, but usually hidden, are the wires connecting the microphone, camera and control console, and the switch box connecting the inside wiring with the outline link to the telephone network. Rooms such as this can either host or participate in ITV classes, and with some imagination can be used for a variety of other applications: faculty or administrator meetings with other schools, parent meetings patched into the local cable-TV network, or teacher in-service training.

Initiating ITV activities is a lot harder than setting up the hardware that makes them work, and in this story are two intersecting policy issues. One reflects current debates in the allocation of resources for public education, the other emanates from the regulatory status of local exchange telephone companies.

If you are a district superintendent who wants to develop ITV capabilities, you cannot typically pick up the telephone and expect help from your state education agency, nor even from the telephone company. When 20 districts in Bergen County wanted to undertake a study of distance learning options, the state-level education officials offered no assistance and showed barely any interest. Unfortunately such a reaction is typical. State education agencies tend to be large bureaucracies that devote considerable resources to enforcing rules and intervening in crisis districts rather than promoting innovation.

As a result, most ITV classroom networks have grown from grassroots efforts — the vision of a local champion or two and a patching together of resources. Among the oldest ITV systems — dating to the early 1970s — is that in Irving, California (Orange County, south of Los Angeles), which was the brainchild of UCLA Professor Mitsuru Kateoka, local educators and the city cable-TV system. Probably the largest of the switched systems is the Minnesota Distance Learning Network, which was developed locally, then, when success was imminent, gained support from state education officials. In fact, people from the Minnesota network provided instruction for Bergen County ITV teachers. Texas is now attempting to develop its ITV "School Link" demonstration sites, a joint project of Southwestern Bell and the Texas Association of School Boards. An excellent report, *Linking for Learning*, from the U.S. Congress's Office of Technology Assessment, provides a summary of distance learning projects.

The educational policy issue is more than one of whether ITV installations are worth their costs, but also one relevant to the nationwide move to consolidate school districts. Often, state and county officials want to consolidate small districts (say, under 2,000 students) so as to gain efficiencies in administrative costs and economies of scale. Whether or not Bergen County officials acknowledge it, for example, investing in ITV was at least partly motivated by their wish to avoid such consolidations. With ITV, districts can share resources without giving up administrative authority or losing local identification with academic programs.

In the case of Bergen County, for example, the districts are reflective of the boundaries of the many small boroughs, most of which have a very strong identification with their specific neighborhood populations. Local boards look in horror at the prospect of losing control of their schools to outsiders, if even a neighboring community.

Texas is another interesting example. Often the rural school district is the key surviving entity in a small town where Saturday night football games are a major community event. In the face of diminishing resources (and population), these small districts welcome any means for survival, and distance learning is one of them. And given some dissatisfaction with satellite-delivered courses imported from distant hosts (problems of differences in course objectives, teaching styles and even regional accents), there is a keen interest in developing ITV networks with neighboring districts. When strategies for planning, financing and implementing ITV networks become available to small districts, we can probably expect substantial growth in that direction, save, perhaps, when consolidation is official state policy.

The telecommunications issues affecting ITV are also difficult, and in some ways are more bureaucratically obsolete than the education issues. When the Federal Communications Commission split up AT&T in 1984, it assumed that while the long-distance markets were increasingly competitive and could be deregulated, the local market was a natural monopoly and, hence, should continue to be regulated.

Today local markets are served by "local exchange" companies, which for a great percentage of the country are parts of the former Bell System. These Bell Operating Companies (or independents like GTE and others) are authorized by state utility commissions to serve specific "local access and transport areas" (LATAs). They provide local and toll services within them, but are prohibited from carrying traffic to other LATAs because that market belong to long-distance carriers. Herein is the first problem of serving an ITV consortium: If the schools involved are not within the same LATA, the local exchange company would have to receive special variances to serve them, and most want to save their requests of utility commissions for bigger and better goals (like rate hikes, for example). Oddly, too, the LATA restrictions can apply to use of satellite-based telecommunications within the local network because they require exchanging signals outside the authorized area. Although some allowances can be made for this if the satellite use is a small percentage of the total traffic, the problem is another illustration of the complexity and obsolescence of current regulation. (Japan already has aggressive plans for a national fiber-based network that will serve a wide variety of public needs, including education.)

Another complex issue arises because local company rates are based on studies of costs and agreed-upon rates of return on investment. When companies include costs of new ITV networks in their rate base, some consumer advocates argue that in so doing they are transferring some of the costs of public education to telephone rate-payers. This, they argue, amounts to a hidden double payment, a fee on top of to property taxes.

The way around this problem is to consider an ITV consortium as a large private customer whose payments will cover the services without cross-subsidies. Costs of linking schools on an optical fiber network are expensive: The Bergen County consortium's up- front share was $1.24 million raised from a bond issue, and each participating school's monthly telecommunications bill can range up to $640.

These regulatory obstacles, added to the fact that most telephone companies have had little or no experience with school networks, makes it all the more unlikely that superintendents will find their local telephone companies enthusiastic or even responsive when they call about ITV options. (Despite New Jersey Bell's current enthusiasm for the Bergen County ITV network, including its highlighting in a public address by President James G. Cullen in November 1990, several organizers of the consortium note that at first it was difficult to get the company interested.) At the same time, ITV service is still relatively new to local telephone companies, which, as regulated utilities, are always worried about getting into touchy legal areas. Also, most of the experiences of both educators and telecommunications providers have been in instructional television applications over the vast distances that separate rural communities, not among metropolitan boroughs. The point here isn't to berate telephone companies on this issue, but to illustrate how the current regulatory environment, as well as the experiences of local exchange companies, are major barriers to planning, pricing and implementing ITV networks.

It must also be said that although the most visible ITV beginnings in the 1970s involved a TV-cable rather than a telephone company, there have been no significant cable initiatives in this area. The five cable companies franchised to serve the area of the Bergen County ITV consortium were neither interconnected nor interested in investing in technology to provide an interactive capability. They were early drop-outs in the planning.

So what are the prospects for ITV? Its strongest suit, we believe, is that educators are discovering its potential and are willing to make the effort for its grassroots development. In a few years we may have sufficient cost-benefit data with which to convince state legislatures to put ITV development into their education budget (which some are considering already). Finally, as local exchange companies become more aware of and able to serve ITV applications, we will occasionally see them taking the lead in such initiatives. After all, the more advanced technology that they can deploy and amortize costs for in the field, the more they can expand their customer bases and new lines of business in what appears to be a climate of continuing deregulation. At the same time, national and state planners might consider pro-active legislation that would not only clear the way for but encourage telephone company (or any telecommunications provider, for that matter) entrance into ITV services.

Meanwhile life goes on in Bergen County ITV classes; this time it's Al McLaughlin teaching the 7:50 a.m. Latin class from Hackensack. As students banter both within and between their classrooms, McLaughlin gives them a copy of an ancient Mesopotamian epic poem that they take turns reading aloud.

> He ordered built the walls of Uruk of the Sheepfold.
> The walls of holy Eanna, stainless sanctuary. . . .
> How Gilgamesh endured everything harsh,
> Overpowering kings, famous, powerfully built. . . .
> Gilgamesh, dazzling, sublime. . . .
> Is there a king like him anywhere?

Reading continues until McLaughlin takes over with a brief lecture on the oral tradition in history — the epic poem, spoken literature — a tradition greatly expanded on by the Romans and eventually rendered into written Latin centuries after the era of this ancient mythological Middle Eastern king. As students leave for a more traditional class, we ask them when they do their declensions and conjugations.

"That's Monday through Thursday," replies a young lady, yellow ribbon in her lapel, looking again at an image of Gilgamesh against a sketched map of the Tigris and Euphrates rivers. "Friday is culture and literature day. . . . we try to make it all real."

"But Gilgamesh. . . ? "

"Hey," she says, "don't you get it? If Mesopotamia is modern-day Iraq, who is the modern Gilgamesh?"

We get it. We also sense that despite the bad press about American education, some of it is doing very well and getting better.

Fred Williams, was a 1991 senior fellow at The Freedom Forum Media Studies Center. In 1991, Victoria Williams was superintendent of the Elmwood Park School District in Bergen County, New Jersey. Both are authors of books on education, including *Growing Up With Computers*.

PART II

Education into the 21st Century

9

Education Issues for the 1990s
An Informal Survey

While the nation waits to see how George Bush will fullfil his promise to be an "education president," the needs of the nation's public schools go largely unanswered. In the Fall of 1990 the *Gannett Center Journal* sent out a questionnaire to leading figures in the worlds of education and media around America. We presented them with one question, simple to ask but infinitely more demanding to answer:

What are the most important educational issues of the 1990s?

The answers we received ranged from single sentences to entire essays, but all of our respondents shared both a commitment to the improvement of American education and the conviction that the media can play a crucial role in that building process. Below we print the responses of six contributors with varied but complementary perspectives on America's schooling as we look ahead to the 21st century.

PEGGY CHARREN
Chair, Action for Children's Television

The education issue most in need of thoughtful media coverage is equity: The inequitable treatment of school populations has harmful effects on poor and disadvantaged children. Inadequate capital investment in economically deprived neighborhoods results in the deterioration of school buildings and the lack of equipment and other resources to stimulate learning through an innovative curriculum and remedial intervention. Inadequate investment in children's health care needs is an even greater problem. We must begin with prenatal care and teach new parents how to be effective educators; we must guarantee that our children are fed and housed and have access to Head Start programs, so that the very youngest students will be ready and able to benefit from public education. These long-range solutions to equity-related problems will require changes in budget priorities at the national, state and local levels, changes that will not happen until the body politic understands why they are necessary for the survival of the nation, and why the "school choice" solution will not solve the inequity problem.

Within the schools themselves, we need to move from a rigid system of rules and regulations to a system based on decentralized authority and decision-making. With school-based management, learning goals are established by principals and teachers working as a team. Flexibility and teacher control encourage curriculum creativity (e.g. adopting new approaches to teaching reading and writing based on current understanding of language and learning). With mutual trust, autonomy and cooperation at the center of school organization, the school becomes a community.

In this decentralized school environment, teachers are responsible at every level, from curriculum development to classroom management. The education of our educators must include not only technical classroom strategies, but leadership skills, the ability to take risks, and an underlying philosophy of learning. We must recognize that the teacher's work day includes preparation, assessment and the opportunity for continued learning. Pay for teachers should reflect their enhanced role.

We need a comprehensive assessment strategy that takes into account a variety of learning styles. We need to develop new instruments to measure students' performance in decision-making, reasoning, communication and other coping skills.

With the decimation of school budgets, corporate involvement in the schools will likely be a major issue of the '90s. We need to encourage public/private partnerships based on sound educational principles that protect the welfare of students. While corporations can certainly contribute resources and expertise to support legitimate educational goals, school-business relationships that provide access to the classroom for commercial purposes (e.g. "Channel One") are a violation of the public trust and should be prohibited.

GEORGE GERBNER
Professor, Annenberg School of Communications,
University of Pennsylvania

*"Media awareness," or "critical viewing," is among the most import-
ant education issues of the next decade.* Liberal education is "liberating
education." It used to mean liberating the young person from unwitting
dependence on a limited and usually parochial cultural environment by
bringing to her or him great art, science, religions and philosophies of
humankind. Today it also means liberation from an unquestioning dependence on the compelling media environment which, for the average
person, encompasses all of culture.

BILL HONIG
State Superintendent of Public Instruction, California

*The cornerstone of education in the 1990s should be a "thinking
curriculum" that must be implemented in every school.* This curriculum
offers every student a rich course content. It requires students to think
and analyze critically so that they are prepared for the future job market,
to participate in our democracy, and to become ethical individuals.

*We need to improve our accountability and assessment programs to
measure more accurately our schools' strengths and weaknesses.* An
effective accountability system should inform policy-makers on the
largest set of available indicators, and include reports of school performance, incentive programs, program quality review, school accreditation
and fiscal management. Our testing system must move away from
multiple choice testing toward judging student achievement on perfor-
mance-based measures that include writing, oral presentations, and
working with other students to solve real-world problems.

*None of our efforts to improve the curriculum will succeed if we do
not implement effective staff development programs.* Teachers and administrators need to learn techniques to encourage team building; en-
hance leadership; encourage each student to excel; and develop active,
cooperative lesson plans. All of this will require substantial time and a
major investment of resources. Importantly, staff development time
should be viewed not as a boondoggle for educators, but as critical an
investment in our schools as training is for successful businesses.

Simply tinkering around the edges will not improve our schools. *Schools must restructure the way they do business.* Simply put, restructuring is broadscale change in how teachers, principals and school districts operate daily to improve student learning. It removes the constraints that get in the way of offering a quality education; keeps the focus on student learning; and empowers professionals to use their best judgment to figure out what works, share decision-making power at the school, and then be held accountable for the results.

We need also to improve high school transitions: Currently, high school students who are going on to a four-year college have a well-defined program. However, students who are going on to work or to a community college after graduation do not. As a consequence, they do not try as hard as they should because they frequently feel that school has little bearing on their future. The business community and schools need to work together to develop a stronger program for these students, one that includes both academic components and technical preparation.

Our youngsters are coming to school with more health and social problems than ever before. Current services tend to be remedial rather than preventive, often resulting in higher costs to address eminently avoidable problems. *Programs for family and youth need to be more effectively coordinated by the various government agencies involved; schools cannot tackle these issues alone, but they are the logical center to coordinate these services.*

JESSE JACKSON
President & Founder, National Rainbow Coalition

We must move away from an unrepresentative Eurocentric curriculum. Such a curriculum does not reflect the universe as it is, so why should the universe perpetuate it? The world is not Eurocentric, the world is multi-cultural and multi-lingual. Why should we teach that which is not the truth? Of the 4 billion people on our Earth, fully *one-half* are Asian. Half of them are Chinese (and they weren't discovered by Nixon). There are 22 nations in the Middle East, most of them Muslim. One-eighth of the human race are African, one-fourth of them are Nigerian. The U.S. and the Soviets between them make up one-eighth of the human race, half a billion people — but there are 700 million people in India alone. Ninety-four percent of the people on Earth are not North Americans. We are only one-third of our own hemisphere. The other two-thirds are our neighbors in South, Central and Latin America, and they speak Spanish and Portuguese, not English. Most people in the world are yellow, brown, black, non-Christian, poor, female, young and don't speak English. That's the world we live in.

By all means let us extract the most valuable truths and findings of the European tradition, but we're part of the world as a whole. One reason why we have these cultural wars is that we cannot read these other cultural traditions. In one of my diplomatic conversations with Saddam Hussein, he started talking about Babylon: a 6,000-year-old civilization just 55 miles down the road from the presidential palace in Baghdad. People who grow up in a 6,000-year-old civilization have a different frame of reference than people whose frame of reference is Valley Forge. They see the world differently; they know that they are a small link in history. Saddam Hussein may wear clothes like ours, but he has a different orientation. We have two different sets of values coming together here, and we need to appreciate that fact in this new world where Saddam Hussein watches CNN at the same time we're watching it.

ANN LYNCH
President, National Parent-Teacher Association

Meaningful parent and community involvement in the entire process of providing education — in the responsibility for developing educational standards and goals and carrying them out — is the most important education concern facing the country today.

We need more parent education so that from the moment a child is born the education process begins. Many people's perception of "restructuring" is that it solves a single problem or enhances a specific goal, but disastrous things can happen if we don't consider the entire spectrum of the educational outcome.

There need to be social changes geared to assisting educational changes. We should learn to look at the child holistically. When we stop treating the child and the family as though school and education were an entirely separate part of their lives, we'll be able to bring about real social changes. The school facility itself needs to be the hub of a child's life. And the social agencies — both private and governmental — need to be brought physically to that school center so that the social needs of a child and of his or her family are met in the same place that their educational needs are met. I envision this not only for urban schools, but for suburban and rural schools as well. This may be a radical opinion, but I believe such involvement is critical.

The nation needs to re-recognize the fact that teachers are professionals. They should be treated with the same respect that we have for physicians, attorneys, judges or university professors. These people are responsible for the most important resources this country has, and they are not respected in their community. Socially they are regarded as somewhere between the middle and lower rung of the community's social strata. You often want to have a professional on your board, and so you seek out a doctor or a lawyer, a university professor or a publisher. You don't seek out a public school teacher. The perception needs to change.

The assurance of equity in all education for all children is a central concern. Entering the "choice process" requires extreme care to ensure that a lot of people aren't excluded. Most people who talk about school choice, in my experience, are talking from the viewpoint of Beaver Cleaver. What do we do about the child who has no choice — because the parent is illiterate, doesn't care, is a crack addict? Or if I want to go to school across town and can't afford to get there, I don't have a choice unless the school district is willing to provide transportation. Or let's say that school X is the school of choice, and it only has room for 10 of the 15 people who want to attend. Rather than that sort of "choice," this country's goal should be to have equity in education to make every school a choice school. The national PTA and I are also opposed to the voucher system because it is the responsibility of the government to provide public education. It is not the responsibility of a government to provide private education. If I opt to send my child to a private school, either for social ranking or for religious reasons, that is something my government should not have to support. I see vouchers or choice money going to private schools as a real infringement on the principle of separation of church and state.

PAUL SIMON
U.S. Senator (Dem.), Illinois

It is time to renew the federal commitment to America's young and old who want to learn. In 1949 the federal government invested 9 percent of its budget in education. Now only 2 percent goes for education (excluding the school lunch program).

Many think that the budget deficit makes this kind of a commitment impossible. I disagree. The double deficit — trade, and the federal budget — means that the federal commitment to the productivity of our people is the most important investment we can make. Without this investment in human resources, the only way to pay off the deficits is with reduced consumption, which means a lower standard of living. A mere 3 percent cut in the Defense budget translates into a 50 percent increase in the budget of the U.S. Department of Education — a move we can certainly afford with the declining Soviet threat in Europe.

The "national education goals" call for all children to start school "ready to learn" by the year 2000. The nation's best hope for meeting this goal is the highly successful Head Start program. Yet the program only serves about 20 percent of eligible three-, four-, and five-year olds. Virtually all Head Start programs have waiting lists. I found out that in Rock Island, Illinois, to meet demand they have one group of children on Monday, another group on Tuesday, another on Wednesday, and so on. What a difference it would make, said the director, if she could serve all of the kids every day. The nation's major federal program for needy children, Chapter 1, is also severely lacking. While the number of children in poverty has grown, the number served by Chapter 1 has fallen. We must do better: It is not enough to set goals. The president must work with Congress to find ways of reaching these goals by directing resources to effective programs.

As the world changes and communications become more frequent, America must increase its competence in international awareness and foreign language ability. This country's deficiencies in foreign language competence and international education have proven to be a roadblock to trade and economic growth. Our future prosperity and security is tied, to a large degree, to our ability to communicate with other nations. We must begin by exposing our children to the languages and cultures of other nations.

An estimated 27 million Americans are functionally illiterate, unable to fill out an employment application or help their children with homework. Ten years ago I held the first hearings in the history of Congress on the problem of illiteracy. Last year the Senate unanimously passed my bill, the National Literacy Act. The National Literacy Act provides the structure, the strategies and the means to mobilize a comprehensive campaign for literacy. It expands and coordinates literacy programs across the country, to focus attention and resources on helping adults, and their children, to learn to read and write.

Media stories on government budgets are not closely watched by the American public. Education, however, is foremost on the public's mind. While people are bored by statistics and dollar amounts, those numbers can be made real by covering the individuals the numbers represent; by showing what a billion dollar increase would mean for the Head Start program; by interviewing inner-city youth who quit college because of the overwhelming loan burden; by featuring successful literacy programs. This nation can and must make a greater commitment to education. The media's responsibility is to help the American public understand the choices that they and their elected representatives are making.

10

National Standards:
The Myth — and Danger — of State and
Local Control

Susan Tifft

In September 1989, I was one of two *Time* reporters assigned to cover the President's Education Summit in Charlottesville, Virginia. As the magazine's sole education writer, I was there to analyze any substance that might come out of the event. My teammate, a seasoned White House correspondent, was there to cover the political angle. He got the better story.

Indeed, despite its historic nature, most reporters — my colleague included — considered the summit more an exercise in political grandstanding and low-cost goodwill than a bellwether of significant change. Being for educational improvement, they said, is like being for motherhood, the flag and apple pie. Who can argue against it? As soon as the governors have packed their bags and the president has choppered back to the White House, everything will remain as it was. Sure, this country has a mediocre education system, but, hey, get real — it's probably not going to change, national goals or no national goals. After all, everyone knows that Americans consider any tampering with the cherished notion of state and locally controlled schools to be akin to a Communist plot. A national approach to education? Never happen, they said. Never happen.

These reporters were right about one thing: There has been a lot of time wasted in the past year and a half arguing over the politics of the president's six national education goals. But they were wrong in thinking that the Education Summit was a throwaway event, or that Americans would never follow the example of their economic competitors — Japan, Germany, Britain, France — and embrace a national approach to education.

According to a 1989 Gallup poll, 70 percent of Americans now favor national achievement standards for public schools and national tests to determine whether students are meeting them; 69 percent say the time is right for — heresy of all heresies — a national curriculum. Whether the farmer in Kansas or the accountant in California admits it or not, state and local control of education, at least in the traditional sense of the term, has gone the way of *McGuffey's Reader*. America is squarely on the road to a national education system and has been for more than a century.

The trend toward a more uniform system of schooling has picked up momentum in the months since the Charlottesville gathering. Educators, politicians and business leaders are practically falling over themselves in the scramble to come up with new and better proposals for national standards, national tests and national curricula. Witness some recent examples:

- In June 1990 the National Center on Education and the Economy (NCEE) recommended that all 16-year-olds take a basic skills test to gain a "certificate of initial mastery" that would qualify them for further education or paid employment. In December, Washington State's Booth Gardner became the first governor to actually propose implementing the idea; at least 10 other governors are considering similar moves.

- The John D. and Catherine T. MacArthur Foundation recently awarded $1.3 million to the NCEE and another education organization to help launch work on a "national examination system" that eventually could be used as the basis for high-school diplomas, college admissions and employment decisions.

- In testimony before Congress in November 1990, National Alliance of Business (NAB) president William Kolberg backed the establishment of national standards, coupled with national assessments, to "ensure that every student leaves compulsory school with a demonstrated ability to read, write [and] compute . . . at world-class levels."

- During a meeting at the White House earlier this year, the President's Education Policy Advisory Committee — a group of 25 business and education leaders — urged President Bush to create a national exam for elementary and high school students.

- In January 1991, Educate America Inc., a new non-profit group chaired by former New Jersey Governor Thomas Kean, proposed that all high school seniors be required to take a nine-hour national test that would cover reading, writing, math, history, geography and science. Students would not "fail" such exams nor would their high school diplomas hinge on them. But results would be sent to colleges and employers as proof of readiness and could be used for state-by-state comparisons of educational achievement.

• For 20 years the National Assessment of Educational Progress (NAEP), the only existing federal exam program, has issued a "national report card" of what the country's fourth-, eighth- and 12th-graders know, but it has never made judgments about what they *should* know. Now NAEP is preparing national standards for its math tests that would rank student achievement as "basic," "proficient" or "advanced." State-by-state results are scheduled to be released in June 1991. If the math test proves successful, NAEP plans to expand to other subjects in 1992 — the first step toward the development of federally administered national standards and national exams. That would go a long way toward meeting one of President Bush's education goals: nationwide tests in grades four, eight and 12 in five basic subject areas.

A decade or two ago, developments such as these would no doubt have prompted charges of un-Americanism. Today, even Reagan conservatives like William Bennett, who as education secretary wrote a book outlining his own ideal of a national high school curriculum, have come to see the benefits of a more standardized approach to schooling.

The main reason for the transformation is fear — something that the media, with its alarmist assessments of America's crime-ridden schools and under-performing students, have helped fan to a hot flame. Unlike Sputnik, which prompted hand-wringing about Communist domination and caused the Eisenhower administration to mainline money into science and engineering programs, the present danger arises not from foreign ideology but from foreign competition. And the enemy? To paraphrase Pogo, it is us.

In an era in which jobs increasingly require brain power rather than muscle power, U.S. students trail their overseas counterparts in almost every subject. According to *Workforce 2000*, a report by the Hudson Institute, between 1984 and the end of the century more than half of the jobs created in the U.S. will require education beyond high school, and a third will be filled by college graduates — 11 percent more than today.

Yet while job requirements are going up, the educational attainment of American students has remained flat or gotten worse. In recent international studies of science and math, U.S. eighth-graders ranked 16th out of 20 in geometry, just ahead of Nigeria and Swaziland. Twelfth-graders were next to last in advanced algebra, ahead of Thailand.

The *average* Japanese student scores higher than the *top* 5 percent of American students in advanced math courses. And little wonder: Only 3 percent of American students take calculus or other advanced math courses. A third of U.S. high schools do not even offer physics.

State and local control is not entirely to blame for these abysmal comparisons, of course. The fractured and harried American family, along with poverty, drug abuse, malnutrition and the Great Satan — television — all share some of the responsibility. Many of the nations with which the U.S. competes also have homogeneous populations and school systems geared primarily to the elite. Our commitment to educate everyone means that we pit a cross-section of our students — the gifted, the average and the deficient — against the cream of the crop in Japan, Hong Kong, South Korea and other countries, skewing test scores in their favor.

But even after discounting for these contingencies, the fact remains that by permitting 50 states and 15,000 local districts to control the nation's schools we have encouraged haphazard educational standards that too often are geared to the lowest common denominator. More young people complete high school in the United States than in most of the countries with which we compare ourselves; the trouble is, it doesn't mean much. "Business has lost confidence that a high school diploma reflects actual skills," NAB president William Kolberg told Congress in November. That might have been defensible when farm work and un-skilled factory jobs were plentiful. Today it is unconscionable.

With major U.S. corporations now competing on a global basis, it seems dangerously out-of-date to maintain one set of standards for students in one state and a different set in another. As newspaper and magazine readers found out after digesting a spate of stories about the 1983 federal report, *A Nation at Risk*, it is indeed the country that is in trouble, not Michigan or Oklahoma. In North Carolina, for example, high school graduation requirements are so low that a youngster who fulfills them but takes no additional math and science courses may find himself unable to meet the admissions criteria of some of his own state's public universities.

Even if economic competition were not a worry, the sheer mobility of modern society would argue for national education standards. Our cur-rent system, developed largely during Reconstruction, presupposes towns and villages made up of families that stretch back generations and rarely leave the place they were born. Such insularity is rare today. How logical is it, then, for a fourth-grader who leaves Duluth for Dallas to confront not only different teaching materials but different academic requirements? Ironically, America has come to expect consistency and high standards in its hamburger chains but none in its schools, where geography is still destiny.

When parents and politicians pound the table against national standards, national tests and a national curriculum, they invariably invoke the country's long history of state and locally controlled schools. But, like the fable of George Washington and the cherry tree, state and local control is largely folklore. In reality, we have been moving toward a more national view of education for a century or longer.

It was the federal government, not states or localities, for instance, that established and ran schools for newly freed slaves and Native Americans after the Civil War, and in 1867 created a central agency to collect information on public education. In 1917 Congress passed the Smith-Hughes Act, which set aside funds for states to implement certain vocational courses — a reflection of the fear that America's workers could not compete with Britain, Germany and other rising industrial giants.

In 1958 Washington took the lead again with the National Defense Education Act, aimed at boosting academic standards in the age of Sputnik. Eight years later the focus turned from the Cold War to the War on Poverty. The passage of the Elementary and Secondary Education Act in 1965 sent dollars flowing to the states; by 1972, the federal government's share of total school expenditures had climbed to 9 percent, the highest level ever.

When President Jimmy Carter made education a Cabinet-level department in 1979, it was a telling indication of the broadening national interest in schools. His successor attempted to reverse the trend, slashing Washington's share of education outlays to 6.1 percent by 1985 — its lowest level in almost 20 years. Reagan also threatened to abolish the Education Department and openly questioned the federal government's expanding role in education. But his was an aberrant view. President Bush has since continued on the course set by Eisenhower, Johnson and Carter, making an as yet unfulfilled promise to be the country's "education president" and convening an education summit that established national goals.

While Washington has been gradually taking a more prominent role in education, states have been smoothing out the financial differences between local districts, setting the stage for a national system of education funding. In the past two years alone, lawsuits in Kentucky, New Jersey and Texas have resulted in court orders to erase the financial disparities that inevitably arise when a district's coffers are dependent on property taxes. Similar litigation is pending in at least 10 other states. Many educators see the efforts to equalize spending within states as warm-ups for the logical next step: equalizing spending between states, a move that would give the United States a school finance system more like that of its counterparts in Western Europe.

Those who argue most vehemently against national standards, national tests and a national curriculum seem not to realize that we already have nationally distributed textbooks that are frighteningly uniform — in their dullness if nothing else — and two national college entrance exams, the SAT and the ACT, that determine what happens in the classroom as effectively as any syllabus dictated by Washington. "It is a myth that education is a state and local matter in this nation," Jonathan Kozol wrote in *Illiterate America*. "Tests are national in use and publication. Test scores are computed on a national curve. . . . Teachers belong to national unions [and] children are educated to regard themselves as U.S. citizens, not citizens of Louisville or Dallas."

What is more, with American eighth-graders spending an average of less than six hours a week on homework but more than 21 hours watching television, a strong argument can be made that students across the country are already learning the same things — they are just not learning things worth knowing. Wouldn't it be better to consciously create national standards and even a national curriculum rather than blindly cling to the fiction of state and local control while private companies produce the national tests, national textbooks and national television programming that make up our present *de facto* national system of education?

School reform in the United States has gone about as far as it can without establishing what constitutes an acceptable level of performance. "It's like an industry that's unclear about its product, and thus is hopelessly confused about quality control," Ernest Boyer, president of the Carnegie Foundation for the Advancement of Teaching, told the Business Roundtable in June 1989.

National goals are fine, but without some clear incentives to reach them or ways to measure progress toward them, they are doomed to be little more than hollow rhetoric. To prevent that eventuality, a diverse array of leaders in education, business and politics now vigorously backs the use of national tests such as the ones administered by NAEP or proposed by Educate America Inc.

At the same time, many Americans resist the standards that national tests imply, as though having clear benchmarks of achievement were somehow undemocratic. The media have not always deepened their understanding. Television, especially, tends to run stories that treat the problems of schooling, job readiness, economic competitiveness, crime, teenage pregnancy and violence in complete isolation instead of showing how one leads to the other.

Americans seem not to realize that in a system in which no one is judged, large numbers of people are bound to fail. It is just such a system that presently allows students to be passed from grade to grade and then on to high school graduation regardless of whether they can read, write or compute adequately to secure a decent job.

A national test, in contrast, would help motivate students to learn by giving them a connection between what happens in school and their future jobs or college choices. It would add meaning to the high school diploma, assuring employers that, whether a job applicant comes from Arkansas or Idaho, he has mastered certain fundamentals. Best of all, says Educate America Chairman Thomas Kean, a national exam would "send a message to all students that hard work pays dividends, that learning is important."

Opponents counter that American youngsters are already among the most over-tested and under-achieving in the world. A national exam, they say, would simply force a child to focus narrowly on a single stressful moment of success or failure and would lead inevitably to the ultimate horror: a national curriculum made up of courses necessary to pass the test.

True enough. But college-bound students already have high-stakes tests — the SAT and the ACT — both of which measure aptitude but indicate little about a student's knowledge or performance. Besides, any national test, however flawed, is surely preferable to the jerry-rigged, value-free system we have now.

A national exam need not be of the multiple-choice, fill-in-the-bubble variety pioneered by the Educational Testing Service. In France, for instance, candidates for high school graduation take written and oral assessments in five areas, including philosophy. In Germany, tests include teacher evaluations and grades as well as oral exams and written tests in math, science, social studies, a foreign language and German. There is no reason why such varied measures of student achievement could not be tried in the United States.

Like the United States, Britain is worried that its blighted schools are turning out young people incapable of competing in the global marketplace. Math is in decline; reading competence is at its lowest level in 20 years. Unlike the United States, however, Britain has begun to make some radical, top-down changes, coupled with some bottom-up modifications in school management. How the transformation ultimately works out may hold some important lessons for us.

In 1988 the far-right Thatcher government pushed through a package of far-reaching reforms that included Britain's first-ever national curriculum. The syllabus, which is now being phased in, calls for mastery of three "core" and seven "foundation" subjects, including math, technology, modern languages and science, as well as national testing at the ages of 7, 11, 14 and 16. All subjects have attainment targets showing what children should know at each stage. At the same time, Britain has introduced open enrollment — or "choice," as Americans call it — and maneuvered around the entrenched elected school bureaucracy by funneling government money directly to schools and allowing teachers and administrators to decide how it is spent.

The key features of the British reform — national expectations coupled with a decentralized approach to school management and decision-making — may strike just the sort of top-down, bottom-up bargain Americans could live with. Setting high standards while at the same time allowing local schools flexibility in how they teach to achieve those standards should give U.S. students clear incentives to do better, but allay fears that Washington is trying to straitjacket teachers and parents or, worse, trample on community values.

Regardless of which model the United States adopts, however, it is critical that the country face up to the myth of state and local control and begin to implement a national education system with thought and consciousness, preserving what works and opening to experimentation the many areas that need overhauling. Most important, Americans should realize that the urgent need to change far outweighs any nostalgia they may feel for an education system that, at present, ill-serves them or their children. As Paul H. O'Neill, CEO of the Aluminum Company of America and chairman of the President's Education Policy Advisory Committee told the *New York Times* in January 1991: "One reason to have national standards is to make sure we change."

Susan Tifft, author and journalist, was an associate editor of *Time* magazine. She was a 1986-87 Freedom Forum Media Studies Center Fellow.

11

Civil Rights:
Roll Over Earl Warren

Michele Magar

Thirty-seven years ago, *Brown v. Board of Education* was hailed as one of the moral and civil rights triumphs of American history. The decision overturned *Plessy v. Ferguson*, the 19th-century legal underpinning of segregation in which the Court had held that a Louisiana statute calling for separate but equal accommodations for white and black passengers did not violate the 14th Amendment's guarantee of equal protection. In classic blame-the-victim style, the Court reasoned that any feeling of inferiority the law caused was "solely because the colored race chooses to put that construction on it."

In *Brown*, a unanimous Court turned *Plessy* on its head by declaring that separate educational facilities were inherently unequal. The decision was the outcome of a 20-year effort waged by civil rights advocates who sought to secure black children access to quality education.

Today some black leaders who seek the same goal believe that separate schooling may be the better way to achieve it, and they argue for educating black males in separate classrooms or schools. The idea has been tried in Miami and Baltimore, and curricula tailored to the needs of black boys are under consideration in Milwaukee, New York and Prince Georges County, Maryland. Separate schooling raises some of the most basic questions facing the country: whether integration has inherent value, whether segregation is inevitably stigmatizing, whether the educational system can address the needs of its most vulnerable population, and what the purpose of education is. For reporters who cover education, civil rights issues have never been more complex.

95

The images that the media captured in the years following *Brown* — the school and college desegregation battles at Little Rock, Ole Miss and elsewhere — are indelibly etched into the national memory. But the agenda facing civil rights and educational activists in the 1990s — less photogenic, perhaps, yet just as vital — has so far failed to produce reporting of comparable intensity or engagement. Perhaps the complexities of the contemporary segregation debate frustrate the media's appetite for dramatic, clear-cut issues, but the need for active and intelligent media involvement is as profound as ever.

Both critics and advocates of separate schooling agree that the problems facing black youth have reached crisis proportions. Consider some statistics: Forty-two percent of black children are poor — more than double the national rate for all children — and black students drop out of high school nearly twice as often as whites. In 1985, black students fared far worse than whites on Scholastic Aptitude Tests: 73 percent scored below 400 on the verbal section; 64 percent performed below that level on the math section. The percentage of white students with scores under 400 were 30 percent for the verbal section, 22 percent for the math portion. In 1989 the national unemployment rate was 5.3 percent, while for black teenagers it was 34.2 percent.

"The education system has miserably failed African-American male children," says Dr. Spencer H. Holland, director of the newly established Center for Educating African-American Males at Morgan State University in Baltimore. "The vast majority who are in jail or on drugs are functionally illiterate. One of their major problems is their lack of educational attainment."

Holland, who says he was the first to propose that young black boys be educated separately from kindergarten through third grade, rests his theory on the importance of role models for children. Many inner-city black children are raised in single female-headed households, with little access to positive male role models, and when they begin elementary school they enter a world where teachers and administrators are predominately female. Holland believes many boys react by identifying school as a feminine activity.

"Research shows that people who drop out of school [tune out] by the end of third grade," Holland says. "You see little black boys of all socioeconomic levels with great desire to learn. By second grade you see something happening. By fourth grade it's like a veil has dropped over their eyes. It's a conscious or unconscious decision just not to pay attention anymore."

Black girls do better in elementary school, Holland says, because they can model themselves on their female teachers and because girls are socialized in what Holland calls "passivity training": "You have to sit down and get your hair done everyday. You learn to keep your head still and sit still, because it won't hurt as much." By the time girls reach kindergarten, Holland says, "they're generally not having any problem with 'sit up straight and tall, stand in straight lines, let's be quiet,'" and that only reinforces boys' belief that school is a feminine activity. The solution to the problem is simple, Holland says: Replace female classmates and teachers with males. Male teachers not only provide examples of successful men, Holland says, they also show boys that school work can be a masculine activity.

But many educators disagree with Holland's premise that role models must be of the same sex and race. "I think we learn from different individuals — both males and females — whether they are of the same religious background, the same ethnicity or racial group," says Dr. Mary Hatwood Futrell. Formerly head of the National Education Association, Futrell is now on the Board of the Quality Education for Minorities Network in Washington, D.C. "Being black doesn't mean I understand all the problems of the black community," she says. "What's important is that I care. It might be more difficult for a white person to relate to a black or Hispanic person, and maybe the attempt will be more successful if you draw from communities which are similar. But we can learn from each other. What's important is that you're willing to make that commitment day after day, month after month. Young people just need something to hold on to."

Futrell also worries that Holland's cure may only worsen the problem. "I'm the first to say the schools and our society have not served these young people well. But by further isolating them, is this going to solve the problem? Or will it say to these kids, in order for you to survive you have to be treated in a different manner?"

Futrell's concern is echoed by Dr. Kenneth B. Clark, a psychologist whose work was cited in *Brown v. Board of Education*. At a press conference opposing the New York City Board of Education's plan to establish a school for black and Hispanic young men, Clark said that "isolating racial and ethnic groups in schools and classes . . . results in inescapable stigma and feelings of inferiority." The plan, he said, "would make our public schools important institutions for the perpetuation of racism."

Addie Johnson says it's one thing to theorize about how best to tackle the problems of black boys, it's another to do it. Johnson is the principal of Robert W. Coleman, an inner-city elementary school in Baltimore. "We're the people on the front lines with the kids every day," she says. "We're the ones who listen to them."

This year Johnson started an all-boy, first-grade class taught by a male teacher. At an elementary school nearby, a group of third-grade boys assigned to a male teacher are in their second year together. The principals of both schools say they've encountered no opposition from civil rights groups or the federal Department of Education. The Department's Office for Civil Rights says there are no plans to investigate the schools, or to develop policy or guidance on the issue of separate schooling.

Johnson says it makes sense to separate young boys and girls, that many boys tend to show off in front of girls and that they're more likely to concentrate on classwork when girls aren't with them. "Girls do better in elementary school than boys," Johnson says. "Girls are not into competition or machismo; they want to do well." Perhaps more importantly, Johnson says, focusing attention on boys is warranted because they're more vulnerable to recruitment by drug dealers: "The street word is you better get these little boys right now — or we're going to get them."

What about stigma? "These kids don't feel that way," Johnson says. "Maybe it's because of their age and maturity level, they don't feel singled out." She says that although it's too soon to measure the academic impact sex segregation has had on the boys, she's already noticed behavioral improvements. "They even hug you now — they're not mean."

Although the psychological impact of separate schooling may be debatable, its legal status is not. In 1987, Pine Villa Elementary School, an inner-city school in Miami with a 98 percent black student body, set up a kindergarten and a first-grade class of black boys taught by male teachers. The program was shut down by the regional civil rights director of the Department of Education, who advised Dade County's school superintendent that separation on the basis of race violated Title VI of the Civil Rights Act of 1964; and that assigning students on the basis of sex for reasons unrelated to safety or privacy was barred by Title IX of the Education Amendments of 1972.

"The law is clear: You can't operate racially segregated schools whether for evil or good," says David Tatel. Currently in private practice with Hogan & Hartson in Washington, D.C., Tatel was director of the Office for Civil Rights at the Department of Health, Education and Welfare from 1977 to 1979. In 1990 he warned Milwaukee's superintendent of schools that the city's plans to open an elementary school and a middle school tailored to the needs of black boys might be illegal. Although the city would maintain a nondiscriminatory admissions policy, Tatel said the schools' focus could be interpreted as discouraging attendance by other students. "In addition to prohibiting an admissions policy that explicitly segregates students based on race, Title VI also prohibits actions which indirectly accomplish the same purpose," he wrote. Despite Tatel's advice, a spokesman for the school district said officials are going ahead with their plans.

Not surprisingly, some civil rights advocates worry that the growing popularity for separate schooling threatens the drive to desegregate schools — and society at large — that began with the *Brown* decision. Social stigma — to which Chief Justice Earl Warren devoted one of the most eloquent passages in his 1954 opinion — remains a critical justification for desegregation, and it was the centerpiece of Thurgood Marshall's dissent in the Supreme Court's most recent school desegregation case, decided in January 1991, *Board of Education of Oklahoma City Public Schools v. Dowell.* In a 5-3 decision (the case was argued before Justice Souter's tenure began), the Court ruled that desegregation decrees may be lifted even if resegregation results, so long as a school district is no longer intentionally discriminating against blacks and "the vestiges of past discrimination had been eliminated to the extent practicable." The Court observed that most of Oklahoma City's elementary schools would be more than 90 percent white or minority without the desegregation order.

In his dissent, Marshall argued that desegregation decrees should not be lifted if doing so would reestablish segregation. "Remedying and avoiding the recurrence of this stigmatizing injury have been the guiding objectives of this Court's desegregation jurisprudence ever since [*Brown*]," he wrote. "Just as it is central to the standard for evaluating the formation of a desegregation decree, so should the stigmatic injury associated with segregated schools be central to the standard for dissolving a decree."

The rub here is that if educators can prove segregation *helps* children, the *Brown* decision begins to totter. But even if it does, proponents of separate schooling for black males face another legal hurdle. Under court doctrine developed from the 14th Amendment's guarantee of equal protection, government classifications based on race are considered suspect. Courts will uphold such classifications only if they serve a compelling governmental interest that cannot otherwise be achieved. With respect to schools, says David Tatel, "You'd have to demonstrate with compelling evidence that a black school is educationally better and that there's no other way to accomplish the same results."

But supporters of Holland's theory point out that court-ordered desegregation decrees have not provided quality education for black youth. White flight to the suburbs and the Supreme Court's bar on city-suburban desegregation remedies have stifled any realistic hope for integration in cities with large black populations. Thirty-seven years after *Brown*, nearly two-thirds of minority children attend schools which are predominately minority, and more than 17 percent attend schools that are exclusively or almost exclusively minority.

"Be realistic," Holland says. "Where are you going to get the white kids to come into these inner city schools? We're dealing with what is — not what ought to be. What the culture has to do is give us African-American educators and leaders an opportunity to say we don't need to be mixed with you to learn algebra."

But even if local governments place schools that purport to serve the needs of black males in areas that are already segregated, as Holland advises, some civil rights advocates say it will turn back the clock on civil rights. "It will legitimize and institutionalize separate schools," says Norman Siegel, executive director of the New York Civil Liberties Union. "When the Rehnquists of the world see this happening, it makes it easier for them to write *Oklahoma* decisions." Siegel says his organization will sue the New York City Board of Education if it implements a plan that discriminates on the basis of race and sex.

Some civil libertarians are also concerned that calls for separate schools for black males could prompt more extreme proposals. "People who don't have good motives could seize on this," warns NAACP Legal Defense Fund attorney Janell M. Byrd. She points to an article in the

November 10, 1990, edition of the Jackson, Mississippi, *Clarion-Ledger* that describes a plan being considered by the Natchez-Adams County school system to establish a "discipline school" for problem youth that would place police officers in the classroom.

Separate schooling for males has also caught the attention of women's rights advocates. Ellen Vargyas, who chairs the National Coalition for Women and Girls in Education, says Holland's theory sends a negative message: Boys are more important than girls. "There's no parallel effort to address the needs of girls," Vargyas says, "yet the drop-out rates are not appreciably different. In every ethnic and income group boys do better than girls on the SATs, and girls face tremendous problems such as teen pregnancy and motherhood. You can't solve the problems of boys in the absence and/or at the expense of girls. They should pursue solutions that are not exclusionary."

Project 2000 is one such solution, and Addie Johnson says her school's participation in the program may account for the changes she's observed in her students. Begun by Holland in 1988 at an inner city elementary school in Washington, D.C., the program recruits male professionals from the community to act as volunteer teachers' aides. Each man is assigned to one class and agrees to spend at least one morning or afternoon there each month, although most come every other week. The idea is to follow the class until it graduates high school in the year 2000. The men perform a variety of tasks: everything from sharpening pencils to one-on-one tutoring. But according to Holland, their most important function is to act as role models for boys.

In Washington the volunteers work with both boys and girls because classes are not segregated by sex. Holland says he created Project 2000 as a compromise after the federal government closed down the all-boy classes in Miami. Since then, he says, the program has spread to St. Louis, Miami, and Patterson and New Brunswick, New Jersey.

Already Project 2000 has shown results. At the end of second grade, after participating in the program for a year and a half, the students in Washington, D.C., took a test in basic skills. According to Holland, the three Project 2000 classes scored between fourth- and fifth-grade levels in math; in concepts and applications one class scored at the third-grade level, and the two others scored at the eighth-grade level.

Whether Project 2000's success is caused by the fact that its volunteers are males or simply because classes have a smaller adult-child ratio that allows each student to receive more attention from teachers is an open question. Asked if the same results could be achieved if Project 2000 used female volunteers, Holland answers this way: "These boys are already overwhelmed by women. They expect women to be the teachers and nurturers. And they expect women to holler at them and that's why they begin to ignore women. When I tell a boy to sit down, he sits down. Mrs. Jones may have to ask him three times. I tell him once."

Project 2000 may prove to be more than just a compromise for Spencer Holland. Because it doesn't involve segregation, Project 2000 may be an approach that civil rights advocates can live with. "If there's an effort to deal with problems affecting black males without ignoring girls, I have no problem with that," says Janell Byrd. "There's a crisis and a need to target help."

As a civil rights reporter, I was initially intrigued by Holland's prescription to improve academic performance by black boys. But as Ellen Vargyas points out, it is not a given that inner-city black boys have had more difficult childhoods or face more serious hurdles than girls. The argument that higher vulnerability to crime and homicide is a greater burden than teenage pregnancy and single motherhood is not only questionable but also misses the larger point that all black children who live in poverty face diminished futures.

Moreover the argument that black boys arrive for their first day at school disadvantaged relative to girls carries a message of hopelessness for black women struggling to keep their families intact in single-parent households. To believe Holland's theory is to believe that no matter what they do, black women cannot give their sons sound foundations. In the same vein, even if one believes Holland's assurance that boys will be made to feel special, what does that mean for girls? Girls already abandoned by fathers must be left behind again while their male classmates are celebrated and ushered into enriched classes just because they are boys.

Most importantly, however, Holland's theory challenges journalists who cover education to think more critically about the purpose of education and what the public needs to know in order to evaluate it. Holland is right when he says that black children don't need to sit next to whites to learn algebra. But journalists need to ask whether mastering a body of skills is the only or even the predominant purpose of school. If it is, what becomes of the vision of school as a crucible for social betterment? In the national debate about educational standards and objectives, it is not enough for journalists to echo the din — not if they are to look intelligently at the substance behind the principles. My own opinion is that Holland's prescription — telling boys they're special and removing them from opportunities to witness female competence — only encourages them to view females as background static rather than peers. It should also raise one's suspicion when solutions are proposed for poor children that parents of middle-class kids would reject, and it is difficult to imagine that middle-class black parents would opt for race- and sex-segregated schooling even if their children were in need of male role models.

All of this is not to say that there is no need for children of both sexes to have contact with professional black males. So long as blacks continue to be disproportionately represented among society's most disenfranchised members, there will always be a need for black role models for children. The success of the children in Holland's Project 2000 program proves that bringing role models into the classroom can be beneficial. But it's important to note that the children achieved those results without being segregated by sex. At least some Project 2000 volunteers should be women. While it's true that teachers and administrators are valuable examples of female professionals, it's also useful for children to see that women can be successful outside female-dominated professions.

Finally, black boys are not the only ones slighted by our nation's education system. Schools should respond to America's increasingly diverse population by using texts and curricula that reflect the contributions of all people and by encouraging a climate that affirms and empowers every child.

Michele Magar is a Washington, D.C., journalist who covers civil rights.

12

Private Enterprise and Public Purpose: Corporations in the Classroom

Joan Richardson

Ray Byers takes a can of Diet Coke from his office refrigerator, then shakes the can furiously.

"I love to do this in front of groups. Once I did this in front of a group of guys from Apple Computer and all the guys in the front row wanted to move farther back," laughs Byers, educational affairs manager for Ford Motor Company, still shaking that can. Finally, he places the can on his desk top and, using a metal pen, gently taps the container all around.

"What I tell them is that you've got to shake things up but you've also got to be careful to contain the action."

Then Byers dramatically flips open the tab and, while a visitor braces for an explosion of brown liquid, grins when only the tiniest amount of fizz spurts out. Byers gamely slurps the offending foam off the top and counsels that "usually it works better than that."

What Byers and his corporate counterparts want to do in education these days is a larger version of his office experiment with Diet Coke: They want to shake up this country's educational system to make American school children fit players in a globally competitive marketplace. Corporate America's obsession with education is one of the most dramatic and far-reaching challenges facing the field today. Every major business group in the country is talking about education, and virtually every major corporation in America is actively involved in trying to make improvements. A recent survey by *Fortune* magazine and Allstate Insurance discovered that 96 percent of executives heading the country's largest corporations think the education system is a problem for the nation.

The business-education connection is a billion-dollar-a-year growth industry, and yet the press has generally failed to translate the importance of this new and growing relationship. If a captain of industry is interested in education, the thinking seems to go, it must only have self-serving or promotional value. At too many newspapers, that means relegating stories about these new partnerships to briefs columns or center-of-the-page feature stories. We have tended to dismiss business' efforts as more evidence of their PR machines at work rather than a sincere concern about improving a system that affects us all.

Part of the oversight lies in the internal turf battles that seem to plague every newspaper — and the larger the newspaper the bigger the turf fights. In this case the war is between the business department and the city desk (which is home to most education writers). Before I became an education writer I was a business editor, and I recall once sitting in a conference room with two other editors trying to sell a business reporter on the idea of doing a story about the growth of business participation in education. Imagine, three editors working on one reporter to get one story done!

Actually what I remember most is her astonishment at the idea that she, a business writer, should do *that* story. It eventually got written, but the episode left me with the lingering feeling that something was wrong. If Lee Iacocca pledges millions to teach children how to read, shouldn't reporters perk up? When Ford Motor Company commits to spending up to $1 million over the next five years to develop an Academy of Manufacturing Science in a suburban high school, shouldn't reporters bang on the doors until they can get in to see what's going on? IBM is putting computers into some urban schools and saying they won't charge the beleaguered districts unless the company can prove that children have learned. But "proved" how, by whom? Learned what, and for what purpose? Doesn't this story deserve closer scrutiny? When a suburban school district says it won't develop a math and science center until corporate contributions are lined up, shouldn't reporters question why the school district didn't do the project on its own if it's so important?

Business is out there spending millions of dollars on public education. It claims to have a deep and abiding concern about the quality of our schools, and that our common economic good hangs in the balance if

American schools are not improved. But are businesses spending their money in the right way? To whom are they accountable for the millions they spend?

Who's watching what's going on?

The growth of business interest in education can be attributed, at least partly, to the Japanese. Battered by a tiny country with few natural resources, America's corporate leaders settled back to take stock in the 1980s. Internally they found fat so they reorganized and downsized. Externally they found fat of a different sort, a mental flabbiness that they believed would affect the quality of tomorrow's workers as well as tomorrow's consumers: Large numbers of American students couldn't read, couldn't add, couldn't think. They found plummeting test scores, heightened anxiety, low self-esteem and little ambition. And they shuddered when they compared what they saw within the blocks and miles of their corporate towers to what Japan's corporate leaders would find in their own country.

So Corporate America determined that education reform must become a priority. But, in nearly a decade of effort, who can show me what business has accomplished in education?

I have spoken with and interviewed dozens of executives about the corporate role in schools. But, I confess that I am still confused about what, exactly, business is trying to do. I know the broad goal: American school children should be globally competitive. They should be the best in the world at math, science, reading and creative thinking. They should be mentally healthy, physically strong and morally alert.

But the millions being spent by business on education have not added up to a prescription for achieving those goals. Company A spends its money on fundamental reading in blighted urban areas. Company B spends its dollars on a model program in the poshest high school in the state. Company C signs up with a coalition of other businesses to encourage children to stay in school. Company D, etc., etc., etc.

So, Corporate America may have identified the problem. But is its focus the correct one? Is it, in fact, a focus?

I wonder if business will be able to effect change, deeply based significant reform, when its efforts are so diffuse. But it's highly unlikely that even America's top corporations will come together to create a single cohesive agenda with specific methods and targets for achieving its goals in 50 different states. Further, given business's inclination to avoid anything that resembles regulation, wouldn't we be foolish to expect business to cry out for someone to provide oversight on its giving to public education?

All the while, money from private coffers keeps pouring into public bank accounts, and no one seems to be calling for accountability. If no one else is doing it, then surely the press must watch and measure what's going on to insure that it's all necessary and that all of this money is being spent to benefit the children. I fear that too many battered school districts are just so happy to receive extra money and any attention that they find themselves unable to exert much discipline when it comes to cashing checks, even when they come with strings attached on how the dollars can be spent.

Some say that the most important contribution that business has made and will ever make to education in America is putting it on the national agenda. "We wouldn't have this round of reform at all if it weren't for business," says Albert Shanker, president of the American Federation of Teachers. Shanker also believes continued business support is imperative to keeping the reform movement alive: "Without a continuing push from business, the reform movement will die."

Harvard University education professor Richard Elmore is one who believes business interest in education will wane as soon as the economy takes a nose-dive, and he compares their forays into school improvement to a "bunch of pick-up games." When business continues to commit resources on the downside of the cycle, Elmore says, that's when he'll be convinced of their sincerity.

That business needs to be involved in education seems clear, even to unionists like Shanker. Business, after all, receives the "product" that the schools produce. If schools were at the top of their game it might be different. Actually, for years, it was different. There was a time when business didn't really want workers who could think, says Charles Thompson, associate dean of education at Michigan State University. And schools largely responded to the needs of business: well-mannered children who learned what they were told to learn and spit it back upon command. America may have wanted doctors, lawyers and even MBAs who could think, but thinking blue-collar employees were not seriously valued by American corporations until the Japanese began to nibble away at their market share. Now even assembly-line workers are being expected to think creatively about how they do their jobs.

The rules in the marketplace changed and schools did not. So business is stepping in to set the agenda for them, to show them what kind of students will be valuable in the workforce.

But the minute the first business indicated it wanted to be "involved" in education, it sent a signal that something was wrong. Business is not merely trying to "help" schools. Corporations want wholesale changes in schools. They want reform of the system.

Business has tackled the education "problem" in a variety of ways. Until recently, the most popular way to partner with a school was through an adopt-a-school relationship in which a business was paired with one school. The business might provide a variety of support tools for the school, ranging from mentoring and tutoring to cookies and field trips. As corporations have begun to experiment with school reform, they've moved determinedly into mentoring programs, programs giving teachers private sector work experience, management training programs for administrators, development of academies aimed at giving students early work-based training and a variety of incentive programs to encourage students to stay in school and get good grades.

In a handful of American cities, major businesses have joined forces to create coalitions, widely known as compacts. Their goal, generally, is to ensure that students who attend school and maintain minimum grades will be guaranteed entry-level jobs or college scholarships. The deal is this: If the schools will deliver qualified graduates, business will deliver jobs. After its first year, for example, the Detroit Compact boasted that 114 high school students who met the standards earned jobs and another 35 were awarded college scholarships.

A casual observer of the Detroit Compact might believe that this coalition between business and education is all about offering hope to children. Not entirely. While jobs and scholarships are wonderful by-products of the coalition, the objective of the Compact is nothing less than reform of the troubled Detroit Public School system. If educators seemed less enthusiastic than their corporate cousins in gushing over the Compact and its related enterprises, it's because they don't relish the thrill of having a pack of MBAs breathing down their necks.

When business leaders caution observers — and that usually translates into reporters — against judging such efforts as compacts too early, they are not talking about judgments based on attendance and GPAs. They're talking about whether their nudging will transform the system.

Now that's an extraordinary expectation, and pursuing it is bound to create resistance and tension. Detroit Edison Chief Executive John Lobbia says that's as it should be. "If there were no tensions, we wouldn't be hitting on the right thing. All we'd be doing is doing more of the same and therefore not creating any change. We don't want to do more of the same. If all we're doing is adding more dollars so they could do more of what they were doing before that didn't work, then we're not getting anywhere. You've got to have some healthy tension," he says.

Reporters, I believe, need to be asking more questions about compacts and other such alliances. They have become Corporate America's preferred way of dealing with public school systems because they demand accountability. Do Americans, as a matter of public policy, want so much private money flowing into their public institutions? Should there be reporting standards required of these corporate efforts, just as businesses are required to report contributions to political candidates because of concern that candidates will be bought off by the extra cash?

The fear, of course, is that Corporate America will begin to stamp its image on the public schools. Executives at all levels dismiss that concern. Corporations, they assure me, want broadly educated citizens. They do not want children who are trained merely to work in a single company or even a single industry. But where is the check to prevent that from happening, especially in the many communities dominated by a single company or industry? We've come a long way from believing that company towns are a good idea. But does this infusion of private capital into public schools raise anew the specter of that sort of relationship?

Compacts and the like also raise questions about the appropriateness of already-beleaguered districts spending their resources to run about creating a system that appeases local corporations. Do compacts create unnecessary work for districts that could better spend their resources directly in the classroom? Do the compact's business partners help underwrite the school district's cost of participation? Does the compact benefit students who would have gotten jobs and scholarships anyway? Are the compacts steering away from at-risk students in order to create proven success?

Whether the business community is participating in a compact or in other types of assistance to education, reporters need to be asking more questions about these programs. For example:

- Determine whether the businesses in your community are truly committed to change or whether their efforts with education are merely promotional. Giving money to schools with no strings attached (whether from business or government) does not make for change. It may be nice and the district may appreciate it, but it doesn't mean the schools are going to get any better. A public company has to answer to its shareholders for how it spends its money, and business reporters ought to question the effectiveness of the way that money is spent. It may not be tax dollars, but it's still somebody's money.

- Many companies say they're involved in adopt-a-school relationships or that their employees "mentor" students. Often the company is lending its name to these kinds of partnerships and does not have much more substantive involvement. The employees, for example, often visit the schools on their own time. Be careful about who gets the credit in these situations. The company should be recognized for being the facilitator, but the employees should get the credit if they're the ones actually devoting the resources — their personal time — to the project.

Business groups have become increasingly critical of adopt-a-school relationships because they do not believe they create change for the system, but adoptive relationships may have value of a different sort. Herman Elementary School in Detroit, a school which draws most of its students from a nearby housing project, has been adopted by a group of employees at Chrysler Corporation's Warren Stamping division in the city. A handful of blue-collar workers visit the school every Tuesday to assist in the classrooms. Many of these children have never known an adult who had a job. They've never had anyone talk to them about the value of work and the fun of having a job to get up and go to everyday. In January 1991, Chrysler treated the students to a day-long visit to the Detroit auto show in downtown's Cobo Center. I find it difficult to criticize any corporate effort that widens the world for underprivileged children, even if the loftier goal of educational reform is not a probable outcome of their effort.

- Check the lobbying record of companies that are vocal in support of improved education. Companies that say they want improved education ought to be lobbying for more than self-serving interests in state legislatures and in Congress. Rather than flexing their political muscle only on issues like emissions or capital gains taxes, urges Ted Kolderie, a senior analyst at the Center for Policy Studies in Minneapolis, executives should focus their energy on tax reform. Kolderie eschews partnerships because they waste limited time and energy and because they do not effect systemic change. Lobbying for tax reform, he argues, could have the greatest impact on making change in urban districts because it would create more equity between urban and non-urban districts.

Companies that want to send a message about the importance of education don't have to spend a lot of money. They can deliver the message as a routine part of their hiring process. Albert Shanker, speaking in Detroit recently, suggested that businesses that hire students for part-time, after-school jobs should begin demanding to see a report card and a note from a teacher saying the applicant does excellent work and could afford to work 15 hours a week without jeopardizing his or her education.

Shanker argues that the word would soon spread that only good students could get jobs. And isn't that the ultimate message that Corporate America wants to spread?

Joan Richardson is an education reporter and former deputy business editor of the *Detroit Free Press*.

13

Choice:
American Values in the Marketplace

Bella Rosenberg

It's hard these days to pick up a newspaper, examine a legislative docket or listen to a presidential speech about domestic issues without coming across the phrase "school choice." These two words are so simple and so evocative of mainstream American values that they hardly get further explanation and don't seem to require it.

But what does "school choice" mean? Is it public school choice, which means that parents would be allowed to choose their children's public school rather than being assigned one based chiefly on where they live? Or does school choice mean permitting parents to use public funds to pay for their children's education at private schools, which get to choose their students, are almost entirely beyond the reach of public authority, and subject only to the rules of the market?

The idea of using public funds to pay for education at private schools has been around under various names — vouchers, tuition tax credits or deductions — for at least 30 years. But for the past few years you could pretty safely assume that school choice meant public school choice because that was the hottest education reform around. Moreover at the beginning of his presidency George Bush embraced public school choice and thereby sent out the signal that the Reagan era's preoccupation with getting private school choices publicly funded was over. After decades of getting nowhere with Congress and suffering all but a few defeats in the states, the advocates of tuition tax credits, vouchers and the like seemed to have called it quits.

Today, however, private school choice advocates are back on our op-ed pages, radios and TV screens, and in our courts and legislative lobbies. And they've made important new friends across the political spectrum — including President Bush, now back in the Reagan fold, and Polly Williams, the former welfare mother and Wisconsin state legislator who ran Jesse Jackson's presidential campaign in the state.

Why is this rather old and frequently discredited idea so newly hot? One obvious explanation is our education crisis and the public's growing skepticism that public schools will reform themselves. But the new enchantment with private school choice is also largely a media phenomenon — the result of a complex social-science book that got the kind of public relations treatment generally associated with a popular best-seller.

The book is John Chubb and Terry Moe's *Politics, Markets and America's Schools*, which, as reporters were fond of pointing out, was published by a reputedly liberal think tank, the Brookings Institution, even though the book advances an agenda generally thought of as conservative. Almost half the book's pages are devoted to statistical analyses that few people are trained to understand but that are crucial to evaluating the merits of its conclusions. Moreover, even prior to its publication the book was criticized by a number of the authors' social science colleagues.

But no matter. With the assistance of a Washington P.R. firm, a slickly readable press release and a major publicity campaign, the book has been widely touted in the popular media and in political circles as "truth." And that is how the private school choice movement was reinvigorated almost overnight: through the rapid spread of the "dramatic news" that Chubb and Moe's study "proves" that school choice — that is, the kind that would privatize education — would substantially improve the academic achievement of American students and thereby end our crisis in education.

What Chubb and Moe are specifically arguing is that the reason for our educational crisis is nothing less than our system of democratic control of public schools. Such a system, they argue, leads "naturally and inevitably" to bureaucratization, and bureaucratization, in turn, works "systematically and routinely" to undermine the development of effective organizations in schools. They also say their study demonstrates that effective school organization is a leading cause of student achievement. It therefore follows that if democratic control is antithetical to developing effective school organizations, then democratic control of schools ought to be abandoned in favor of market control. Public schools, Chubb and Moe conclude, "must be freed from the political institutions that now control them and be subjected to the discipline of the market. Ultimately this is what makes private schools work, and it can make public schools work too." They call their recommendation "public school choice," but it more closely resembles a publicly funded private school system.

No wonder the media and politicians are taking notice. This is bracing and powerful stuff. If Chubb and Moe are right, America's long struggle to find the keys to school improvement and high student achievement may be over. Democratic control of schools is our problem, and market control is "the panacea," as they call it.

The question is, are they right?

It is easy to agree with Chubb and Moe's argument that bureaucratic rules and regulations — and the resulting lack of autonomy — inhibit the development of effective school organizations. In fact, this argument figures prominently in the most recent stage of the public education reform movement, where it has been producing some loud and overdue calls for officials to put an authoritative broom to the piles of bureaucratic red tape littering our schools. It is behind the movement to "professionalize" or "empower" teachers. It informs the latest round of decentralization efforts. It is the rationale for experiments with school-based management and shared decision-making. And it is the foundation of recent discussions about establishing standards for students and outcome levels for schools, experimenting with incentives and leaving virtually all professional decisions about education in the hands of school personnel.

One would think that Chubb and Moe would approve of these developments, consistent as they are with their beliefs about effective schools. And they do mention a number of them approvingly. But in the final analysis, they say, these efforts will fail. The officials of a democratically controlled school system may grant greater autonomy today, but they are sure to withdraw it tomorrow, or whenever the first complaint or problem materializes.

Now, there's no question that our *particular* system of democratic control of schools is deficient. But that's not what Chubb and Moe are saying. Their argument is that democratic control *per se* is responsible for ineffective school organizations, so we must shift to market control.

This is a rather large and astonishing leap, since there are many different ways to govern schools democratically, and therefore many possibilities for reform short of market control. Moreover if democratic control is the root cause of our educational crisis, then why are Japan's or West Germany's democratically controlled and highly bureaucratic school systems among the most successful in the world?

Many of the problems Chubb and Moe attribute directly to democratic control may instead be the result of the unusually accessible and politically vulnerable position of public schools in our particular education governance system. Public education is a state responsibility, but schools are simultaneously controlled by local school boards, state legislatures and departments of education and the federal government. Moreover our school politics, unlike those in most other advanced democracies, are not tempered by meaningful, professionally defensible, local, state or national educational standards because we have never accepted the idea of reaching a common understanding of what our students should know and be able to do (though this may be changing). All of these features of our present system are, of course, reformable without resorting to market control. To pretend, then, as if we either have to live with the poor performance of our present public schools or plunge into the uncharted waters of market schools is not only dangerous, it is irresponsible.

It also doesn't add up to much of a theory. If, as Chubb and Moe say, democratic control inevitably produces bureaucracy, ineffective school organizations and poor student achievement, then we would expect it to work pretty much this way in all of our public school districts. There are other holes, too, in Chubb and Moe's all-embracing implication of democratic control for the crisis of our nation's education. Suburban school districts, for example, like urban and rural districts, are subject to democratic control. And yet, while a number of them now have large central bureaucracies, as urban schools do, most do not. And rural school districts definitely do not. Suburban schools, Chubb and Moe also tell us, tend to have more effective organizations and higher student achievement than urban and rural schools. Why does democratic control work differently and with different effects in urban, rural and suburban school districts?

The answer Chubb and Moe give is instructive: Democratic control works only in homogeneous or problem-free environments.

> The nation's large cities are teeming with diverse, conflicting interest of political salience — class, race, ethnicity, language, religion — and their schools are plagued by problems so severe, wide-ranging and deeply rooted in the urban socioeconomic structure that the situation appears out of control and perhaps even beyond hope. . . . The fact is, suburban schools are lucky. They are more likely to be blessed with relatively homogeneous, problem-free environments, and, when they are, their organizations should tend to benefit in all sorts of ways as a result. Urban schools do not look like suburban schools because urban environments do not — and in the foreseeable future, obviously will not — look like suburban environments.

To those who value America's diversity and pluralism and who believe that it is extreme poverty rather than heterogeneity that bedevils its cities, this is shocking stuff. It does, however, help explain why Chubb and Moe reject democratic control of schools and insist that market control is the only solution: because markets, by their very nature, strive to sort diverse individuals into homogeneous groups. This is not a matter of opinion; any economist or businessman will say it is a fact. This is how markets are supposed to work. By its very nature, then — and not by overt discriminatory policies — market control of schools would tend to separate students by class, race, political power, level of achievement and behavior.

Private school choice proponents like Chubb and Moe give this divisive element of markets a benevolent spin: Because market schools can stake out a particular niche, they are more able to "please" their clients, "satisfy" them, "fulfill" their "interests," "tastes," "needs" and "wants." What they are also saying is that we ought to turn the historic ordering of social and individual values in public education upside down: that the purpose of taxing American citizens for education should be to fulfill private interests rather than, or only incidentally to, pursue the public interest. They observe disapprovingly that democratic control forces public schools to try to be all things to all people, and they tell us approvingly that private schools are under no such obligation: They must merely please their targeted segment of the market.

But how is this done in private schools? Market schools, like market economies, differentiate by product and price. But private schools also get to choose their customers. Thus, while anyone whose need or taste in cars runs to Rolls Royces can buy one so long as he can pay the price, not everyone who can afford the price of a particular private school can get in. You may have to be the right religion; you may have to be a high achiever; you may have to produce evidence that you're not a discipline problem; you may have to pass muster as someone who can "fit" with the school's philosophy, curricular emphasis or existing student body. To be sure, unlike the Rolls Royce customer, you may not have to be able to afford the price of tuition because you may be able to get a scholarship. But you *must* meet the school's objective and subjective admissions criteria.

Is this public school choice or privatization at public expense? As Alice's experiences in *Through the Looking Glass* remind us, words can be made to mean whatever you want them to mean. So casting aside distractingly charged words like "public school choice" and "privatization," what exactly do Chubb and Moe mean? "Our guiding principle in the design of a choice system," they say, "is this: Public authority must be put to use in creating a system that is almost entirely beyond the reach of public authority."

According to Chubb and Moe, local arms of a state "choice office" would give public or private schools "scholarship" money based on the number of students that chose them (and were chosen by these schools); scholarships would be an aggregate of local, state and federal funds. Chubb and Moe then make some worthy recommendations for an equalization approach to funding that would guarantee students in all districts, and not just wealthy ones, "an adequate financial foundation." They even recommend that, for the sake of equity, parents not be allowed to supplement their children's scholarships with personal funds and that students with special educational needs be given larger scholarships.

But then they begin to backtrack. "Complete equalization," they say, "strikes us as too stifling and restrictive. . . . The citizens of each district can be given the freedom to decide whether they want to spend more per child than the state requires them to spend. They can then determine how important education is to them and how much they are willing to tax themselves for it. This means that children from different districts may have different-sized scholarships."

What this really means is that even if poor and wealthy districts value education equally and tax themselves at the same rate (a hardship for poor districts), the result will be fatter scholarships for children from wealthy districts.

There is an additional way that this new "public" school system would be allowed to differentiate according to price: Schools would be permitted to "set their own 'tuitions.'"

They may choose to do this explicitly — say, by publicly announcing the minimum scholarship they are willing to accept. They may also do it implicitly by allowing anyone to apply for admission and simply making selections, knowing in advance what each applicant's scholarship amount is. In either case, schools are free to admit students with different-sized scholarships, and they are free to keep the entire scholarship that accompanies each student they have admitted. This gives all schools incentives to attract students with special needs, since these children will have the largest scholarships. It also gives schools incentives to attract students from districts with high base-level scholarships. But no school need restrict itself to students with special needs, nor to students from a single district.

Much like private schools, then, the new "public" schools would be able to differentiate not only by product but through price. And, by the inherent logic of the market, they will differentiate in other ways as well. Market schools will recognize that children with special needs cost a lot to educate, probably even more than the amount represented by the "larger scholarships" such children would carry. Or if they believe they can do this within costs, the thought will occur to them that if they cut down on services they can use student scholarship funds for other purposes, like advertising for more students or supplementing staff salaries or buying nice furniture — all of which would be perfectly legitimate and undetectable in this unregulated plan. Or they may decide that it does not pay to attract students with special needs at all, no matter how large their scholarships, because doing so may repel students with higher base-level scholarships, who are likely to be from wealthier districts and thus likely to pose fewer problems and challenges and be less costly to educate. But they'll note that public funds carry with them an obligation to observe nondiscrimination laws, so if they want to avoid trouble they had better be circumspect about rejecting students who fall under the protection of those laws. (Though in the closest thing to Chubb and Moe's plan we have, the Milwaukee choice program that includes private schools, private schools were exempted from having to accept students with special needs, a decision that was upheld by the federal Department of Education.)

But many of these schools would quickly realize that they wouldn't face this issue if those students never sought admission in the first place. And so if the niche these schools carved in the market did not explicitly extend to those students and their advertising and other materials were not targeted at them, this group of children would be less likely to show up. On the other hand, there are bound to be some "public" schools that will decide their niche is serving some category or other of students with special needs, and they will aggressively pursue this "market." There may even be some "public" schools that decide their niche is offering a common school experience, where children of all classes, races and creeds sit side by side and learn through a common curriculum. This, however, is not likely to be typical; the incentives in market schools are lined up in the opposite direction, and there is nothing in our historical experience to suggest that consumer demand would turn this around.

The question then is, wouldn't this "uncommon" school result be strictly an accidental or natural by-product of the exercise of individual choices by students and parents? And wouldn't it thus be compatible with our belief in individual liberty and therefore legitimate?

Perhaps. But an unspoken and central feature of market school choice is that students and parents are not the only ones making choices; the schools also get to choose their students.

> Schools will make their own admissions decisions, subject only to nondiscrimination requirements. This is absolutely crucial. Schools must be able to define their own missions and build their own programs in their own ways, and they cannot do this if their student population is thrust on them by outsiders. They must be free to admit as many or as few students as they want, based on whatever criteria they think relevant — intelligence, interest, motivation, behavior, special needs — and they must be free to exercise their own, informal judgments about individual applicants. . . . Schools must also be free to expel students or deny them readmission when, based on their own experiences and standards, they believe the situation warrants it (as long as they are not 'arbitrary and capricious').

And what happens to the leftover students, the youngsters whom no schools want? They will get the leftover schools, the schools that few students and parents want.

The "public" school choice plan that Chubb and Moe are recommending is therefore more typically, and accurately, known as privatization at public expense. There is little in it that is public and nothing at all that respects the historic role and social ideals of public education in a democratic society. Of course, Chubb and Moe might dismiss this observation as the defensiveness or blinkered vision of public school advocates. Yet it is consistent with their own explicit rejection of any higher purpose for public education. The problem, at least for them, is that about 200 years ago this nation decided that public schools were *supposed* to have a transcendent purpose. That is why America created a public school system financed out of public funds in the first place, and that is why public schools were placed under direct democratic control;

not only to enable individuals to pursue their particular academic and vocational interests in education, but, first and foremost, to pursue the public interest in education. Some of those values have remained consistent over time, while other have changed or been elaborated to include Americans once excluded from the vision of equal educational opportunity. But this fundamental principle and rationale of free public education in America has endured.

That conception of public education, Chubb and Moe believe, has outlived its usefulness. Indeed, that is the most significant and radical message in their work, and it comes to us wrapped in the authority of a scientific proof, namely, that democratic control undermines effective school organization, the leading cause of student achievement. The question is, even if we concede to Chubb and Moe their argument about democratic control, have they proved that effective school organization is the leading cause of student achievement?

Despite their obvious fascination with the book and its scientific authority, few commentators in the popular media have bothered to ask anyone whether Chubb and Moe's analysis of school organization withstands scrutiny. As many of Chubb and Moe's social-scientist colleagues, among others, would have said, it does not; it certainly does not "prove" that market control will dramatically improve education. For one, the database Chubb and Moe use was already under a dark cloud, and the way they use it exacerbates its problems. They relate the achievements of high school students in 1980 and 1982 to information about the organization of these students' schools in 1984, two years after the students had left. Second, their statistical techniques are, at best, unconventional; their methodology gives private schools an advantage; and most of the time they don't tell you if they're analyzing private or public schools, let alone which types of public or private schools. Moreover what Chubb and Moe — and now everyone else — call high school "student achievement" is actually a very narrow measure: the results of a 116-question, 63-minute test that is insensitive to the diverse curricula that characterize our diverse high schools.

These problems aside, what did Chubb and Moe find? First, that the average gains registered by students between their sophomore and senior year was shockingly small — 6.6 more questions answered correctly on a 116-item test. Now, small test-score gains are not promising breeding grounds for bold policy recommendations and media headlines. But, voila, the issue of small gains disappears from Chubb and Moe's discussion because they transform the number of correctly answered test questions into *years* of student learning.

Thus, the average student test-score gain, a mere 6.6 additional correct answers between the sophomore and senior years, becomes two years of student learning; the 4.66 fewer correct answers given by the lowest student quartile group become a *loss* of 1.4 years of learning; and the average gain of the highest student quartile group, 18.13 additional correct answers, becomes 5.46 years of learning accomplished during the last two years of high school. And in the end the difference between the highest and lowest student quartile group is a staggering 6.86 years of learning!

That is how very small average test-score gains become dramatically large differences in student achievement and school performance. That is why Chubb and Moe's results look like "major" findings with "profound" policy implications. And that is how a book that devotes almost half its pages, not counting the statistical appendices, to quantitative analyses that few people are trained to understand becomes the hottest and most covered educational "news" in the popular press.

The big surprise after all is not that Chubb and Moe prove their hypothesis but that they fail to make the case that student achievement is largely caused by school organization. In fact, *all* the variables they put in their model to explain student achievement taken *together* don't explain more than 5 percent of the variation in student achievement. And when an analysis that can account for only 5 percent of what it is trying to explain is used to tell us that school organization has the same impact on student achievement as family background, or that school organization is twice as strong an influence on student achievement as the makeup of the school's student body, then we are being told virtually nothing at all; twice almost nothing is still almost nothing.

Clearly, these problems cast a long, dark shadow over Chubb and Moe's conclusion that being in an effectively organized school would yield the average student an additional one-half to three-fourths year's worth of achievement. But casting even these problems aside, what does this conclusion mean? The gap in achievement between the lowest and highest student quartile groups was 6.33 years, so the effect of school organization on closing that gap — about a half year — is very modest. Moreover, if we return to what "years" of student achievement really means, one-half to three-fourths of a year is no more than one or two more correct answers on a 116-item test. And when Chubb and Moe control for the effects of students' curriculum track (academic vs. general or vocational), 30 percent of the influence of school organization on student achievement disappears, leaving the average student one more correct answer, or a fraction thereof, on a 116-item test. Is this solid ground for embracing market control of schools? Does this constitute proof, as private school choice proponents claim, that private schools outperform public schools? And does this merit the media's treating *Politics, Markets and American Schools* as if it contained the cure for cancer?

No one seriously expects reporters to examine complex statistical analyses to see if they support the test of a press release or news conference. However it is not unreasonable to expect them to check with someone who can. Sure, listening to explanations of quantitative analyses may make one's head ache. But failing to do so when writing about controversial material that stands or falls on its numbers means turning the public's head, and often in an unsupportable direction.

The problem is exacerbated, of course, when reporters pit "objective" research against the "opinions" of the group that the research presumably discredits. This is in fact a popular sport in education reporting, and a number of researchers, among others, now know how to initiate it by declaring that their findings will be anathema to the education "establishment." The routine is frustratingly predictable: A reporter calls a representative of the education "establishment" for a comment on a press release that claims such-and-such proves something. The representative tries to respond in the same research-based language as the study, but that's not what the reporter wants to hear. Moreover by virtue of working for an interest group rather than a think tank or university, the representative's counter-analysis is often considered politically and intellectually suspect. The reporter persists; a controversial and pithy rejoinder is what he or she is after, and eventually one is forthcoming: defensive-sounding "opinion" contrasted to objective research, the survival of our limping public education system vs. "proof" of dramatic gains in student achievement if we embrace school choice.

If school choice is going to become more than an ideological mantra, the news media need to start thinking more critically about what it means and whether they are reporting on public school choice or on plans for publicly funding schools that are "beyond the reach of public authority" and that get to choose their students to boot. They also need to start treating evidence as something that ought to be checked out rather than swallowed whole. And a good place to start is with the so-called no evidence that we would boost student achievement if America abandoned the distinguishing political and social values it embodied in public education and embraced private school choice.

Bella Rosenberg is the assistant to the president of the American Federation of Teachers.

PART III
Book Review

Brain Checking

Gerald Grant

Small Victories: The Real World of a Teacher,
Her Students, and Their High School
by Samuel G. Freedman (Harper and Row, 1990).

Lives on the Boundary: A Moving Account of the Struggles
and Achievements of America's Educational Underclass
by Mike Rose (Free Press, 1989, Penguin Books, 1990).

Escalante: The Best Teacher in America
by Jay Mathews (Henry Holt and Co., 1988).

Among Schoolchildren
by Tracy Kidder (Houghton Mifflin, 1989).

Contradictions of Control: School Structure
and School Knowledge
by Linda M. McNeil (Routledge and Kegan Paul, 1986).

In the flood of reports on educational reform issued over the last decade we have heard from nearly everybody except teachers. Presidential commissions, foundations, corporate leaders and scores of researchers and scholars have diagnosed the ills of the American educational system, but the voices of teachers and visions of good teaching have played a less salient role in the debate. It's in the nature of reform reports to attend to policy questions and to look at trends and aggregates. Why would you want to spend a year or more in close observation of one teacher? What does a sample of one tell you? Whether good or bad, it can be dismissed as atypical. Putting Linda McNeil's book aside for a moment, what we have here is a sample of four, three of them portraits of exceptional teachers by sensitive observers who spent months in their classrooms, and the fourth an autobiography by a gifted teacher, Mike Rose. While such a sample may not be scientific, the collective portrait that emerges tells us more about the real stuff of teaching and learning than can be found in a roomful of reform reports. The struggles these

teachers waged to educate some of the poorest children in the United
States also reveal deep truths about what ails us.

On the one hand, these are success stories. In *Small Victories*, Samuel
Freedman gives us a stunning life of Jessica Siegel, who teaches English
at Seward Park High School on the Lower East Side of New York, which
teems today as in decades past with immigrants who mostly do not speak
English. Jay Mathews apologizes for the subtitle of his book, *Escalante:
The Best Teacher in America*, fearing it may embarrass his subject. But
Mathews is not the least abashed in explaining why he was right to choose
that description for a man who brought national honors in calculus to a
school in Los Angeles that had been taken over by gangs and where most
students had never heard the word calculus. Chris Zajac is an inspiring
teacher of fifth-graders in the "Flats" of Holyoke, Massachusetts, a
rundown neighborhood of old mills and factories, and Tracy Kidder's
loving portrait takes us inside her classroom and eventually inside the
hearts of her children. Each of these books is in part a love story of
teachers who love their craft and love their pupils, and in part Horatio
Alger stories. As Mike Rose puts it in recalling his work with the least
advantaged, with those who lived *Lives on the Boundary*, he had been
trying to create an Honors College for the underprepared. People might
smile about such a description, but "as our students would have said, we
were serious as a heart attack."

How do teachers show they love children? First they get to know them,
because good teaching is an encounter between persons. Jessica Siegel
began her classes by eliciting autobiographies of pupils. And she wanted
them to get to know her as well, so she asked them what expectations
they came with and what they thought a good teacher was like. Some are
bargaining with this first assignment: "My expectation is that Ms. Siegel
will be a teacher give the students less homework. . . . " Others are quite
direct about the contract they have in mind: "What I really want from
English is to learn and pass the course." (What "passing" means and
whether it has much to do with genuine education is a subtext that runs
throughout these books and is the main text of Linda McNeil's more
sociological treatise.) One student has thought about how good teachers
motivate and engage you: "I expect a teacher to keep a student involved.
I expect her to do this by having fun and interesting lessons that are not
just lectures. There must also be a little comedy in the lessons, which will

keep us awake. A teacher must be understanding of her students' problems."

Knowing students means divining their pains and possibilities, sensing hidden treasures they may not even suspect are there. Jessica Siegel exploited that knowledge to produce students who wrote prize-winning articles for the *Seward World* about drug and gang wars and about gentrification movements that forced them out of housing that was suddenly becoming desirable to real estate speculators.

Mike Rose believed that establishing connections with students was at the heart of all good teaching. He had been a poor boy who came from the streets, and he knew all the insecurities that plagued youngsters who didn't know how to enter the conversation or to make the intellectual moves that kids raised with Encyclopedia Brittannicas did. He modeled his own teaching on the teachers who had touched him, who knew how to guide him into "conversations that seemed foreign and threatening, . . . showed you how to get at what you don't know." They were teachers whose deep joy for poetry fused with their love of human community. They touched you, looked into your eyes when they talked to you, made moments to break bread together. They tolerated a lot of failure that they saw as necessary steps to success. They knew that learning to write meant "you'll miss the mark a thousand times along the way," yet developing writers will grow through botched performances "if they are able to write for people who care about language, people who are willing to sit with them and help them struggle to write about difficult things."

Rose shows us how teachers often misperceive failure, concluding that incorrect answers are evidence of low ability when they are really the result of different patterns of reasoning. He wants us to look for the intelligence that may lie behind the error, as with a student who explains that she wrote a sentence fragment as a way to vary sentence style. She learns how to do that without writing fragments, but it's important to see the intelligence of her intentions.

But these teachers did not let awareness of the pains destroy high expectations. They were not sentimental. Early in the term Escalante would greet many students who had not yet become accustomed to his expectations, "Good morning. Nice to see you. You're still failing." Or they might not get through his door if they failed to answer a question about last night's homework. They would be quarantined in the hall with directions to study page x for 10 minutes, when they would have a second chance to gain entry. Seniors and their parents had to sign a contract that they would spend hours after school and some Saturday mornings in special tutoring sessions. Siegel hangs tough when a student whines he has nothing to write about: "Just put your pen on paper. Something will come." Each of these teachers exuded compassion, but they also clearly established their authority. Here's Chris Zajac jacking up her fifth-graders, most of them poor and Puerto Rican:

> Mrs. Zajac wasn't born yesterday. She knows you didn't do your best work on this paper, Clarence. Don't you remember Mrs. Zajac saying that if you didn't do your best she'd make you do it over? As for you, Claude, God forbid that you should ever need brain surgery. But Mrs. Zajac hopes that if you do, the doctor won't open up your head and walk off saying he's almost done, as you just said when Mrs. Zajac asked you for your penmanship, which, by the way, looks like you did it and ran. . . . Clarence. Mrs. Zajac knows you didn't try. You don't just hand in junk to Mrs. Zajac. She's been teaching an awful lot of years. She didn't fall off the turnip cart yesterday. She told you she was an old-lady teacher.

They all have their moments of yelling, cajoling, persuading, and occasionally shaming or stinging to wring a performance from students. They hound them, call their parents and guardians. Escalante confronts parents who keep their daughter waitressing at the family restaurant too late to do her homework. Although they are ambivalent about his college aspirations for her, they agree to reduce her hours. Siegel drives three students through a snowstorm for appointments she has wangled with an admissions officer at SUNY-New Paltz, even though these students fall below the grade-point average of 75 stipulated for the special program for economically disadvantaged students for which they have applied. But she has steered some other students New Paltz's way and they have done well, so the admissions officer relents. The students themselves have strong self-doubts about whether they are "college material," and one of them comes to her office an hour late, and then without his application forms. So she waits for him to retrieve them from home, the storm gets worse, they make a wrong turn, they arrive at New Paltz as the office is closing and there's no interview. She's disappointed, but she pulls herself together, takes the students to meet a Seward Park alumnus for a tour of the campus and drives home with a sore throat and a headache. Many weeks and letters of recommendation later one of the students wins admission to New Paltz, one to Vermont and the third to SUNY-Binghamton.

As we have just seen with Mrs. Zajac, each of these teachers has a style, a presence, a persona. Escalante learns the names of feared gang leaders from a counselor friend and casually drops these into his classroom conversation. He pretends to know many gang secrets and the students love it. He has a long list of affectionate nicknames for students — a "Rajneesh" is a student who wants to get an A without doing anything, a "Hyatola" one who comes in the classroom and just sits. They are not afraid to be a little crazy, to let go. Jessica Siegel dresses in clashing neon colors while Escalante favors dull brown and black suits. But both have an intimacy with students based on their willingness to reveal themselves in the classroom and to open themselves to challenge as they push students to question their own assumptions.

Demands in their classrooms are high, but students also see that these are teachers who have high expectations of themselves, who put in 14-hour days and who say by their availability to students after school and on Saturdays that I know you can learn and I am here to help you succeed. They establish a coaching rather than an adversarial relationship with students. Escalante is most conscious about this. He literally makes his students feel they are teams who are preparing with him for a big contest against an external foe — the Advanced Placement exams administered by the Educational Testing Service in Princeton, New Jersey. Both teacher and student are being judged, and they develop an *esprit de corps* as they prepare for the challenge. His students wear calculus jackets and classes often begin with warm ups in which students beat their hands on the desks and sing popular song lyrics such as "We are the Champions. We will rock you." These teachers encourage cooperative learning in which students work in teams and tutor each other. In a variety of ways they provide a scaffold of support that students know they can rely on.

Most of what we have been discussing thus far are the moral qualities of good teachers — their perseverance, caring, courage, and their attempt to provide true equality of educational opportunity. For the most part they were deeply knowledgeable, although Mrs. Zajac admitted her fifth-graders may have suffered because she didn't shine in math herself. What made them exceptional teachers was the way they put that knowledge at the service of students. What is most important is not what you know, said Escalante, but what is transmitted. These were teachers who reflected deeply on their aims and on ways to connect with students, to motivate and engage them. They were close students of their craft and creative about the techniques of teaching.

How would you encourage writing among 15 students classified as the poorest readers among the fourth- and fifth-graders in a urban elementary school serving working-class families? You will have them once a week for an hour after lunch at a table in the corner of the cafeteria. Soon they come walking in the door "in scuffed pumps and knee socks, print dresses, sneakers and pants stained with grass, the odors of milk and exercise." They are quiet. Some look apprehensive. Mike Rose has thought about this encounter. He gets them to pull up around the table and talk about themselves and their friends and hobbies and pets. Then he asks, "Do you ever watch people? You know really look at them and wonder about them? Well, here's three I want you to look at." He tapes three pictures to the wall: one of John F. Kennedy, another an advertisement he had clipped from an old *Life* magazine showing a lonely girl looking out of an apartment window, and a "particularly grungy photograph of Ron McKernan, aka Pig Pen, the hirsute keyboardist for the Grateful Dead."

He asked them to take turns talking about the pictures. "What did they see: What did they think each person was thinking? What would these people have to say to each other or to them?" Then he asked them to pick a picture and write. Next week he has an exercise on "snazzy words": eulogy, lampoon, paranoid. He has written the words on big placards. Kids get to pick one that sounds snazzy to them. He talks with them about what that word means. Then they draw from a pile of pictures one that they think expresses that word and write why. After they leave he types up their sentences and pastes each child's contribution in the center of a sheet of colored construction paper and tapes the sheets to the wall of the cafeteria. The next day he notices them pulling friends over to show what they have written. Another week he plays Paul McCartney's comic country-western ballad "Rocky Raccoon" and lifts the needle just as Rocky Raccoon is about to bust the door down to confront his runaway lover. He asks the kids to write their own endings to the song. By the end of the year each child's writing has been collected and bound as a small volume that a friend of Rose's with a gift for calligraphy has provided with a cover labeled "Joey's Book" or whatever the child's name may be.

Obviously these are "techniques" that change lives. Years later Rose is teaching a class of veterans, many of them high school dropouts, who had returned from Vietnam. Willie Oates, a heavily muscled bald man with a gold ring in his ear stared silently at him from the back row. Rose had been trying to prepare the vets for college entrance and had organized his class around the skills of summarizing, classifying, comparing and analyzing. In the first class he gave them 20 unlabeled paintings of the human body, from Michelangelo to cubist abstractions, with instructions to group them any way they wanted. At the end of the fourth week Willie Oates came slowly to the podium. He had not yet spoken in class. He pounded on the podium in cadence with his speech: "You-are-teaching-the-fuck-outta-me." And in another class he met Olga, a heavily mascaraed older woman who fought him all the way on *Macbeth*. "How do you expect us to *read* this stuff?" But he sat with her, "took her through a scene, paraphrasing a speech, summarizing a conflict. Sometimes I'd force her to direct her anger at the play, to talk at it, make her articulate exactly why she hated it, be as precise as she could be. . . . " One day she told him, "You know, Mike, people always hold this shit over you, make you, . . . make you feel stupid with their fancy talk. But now I've read it, I've read Shakespeare, I can say I, *Olga*, have read it. I won't tell you I like it, 'cause I don't know if I do or I don't. But I like knowing what it's about."

These teachers continued to be engaged in inquiry and learning themselves. Rose went back to college to sit in on classes as he figured out ways to teach these courses and put together his own textbooks. Jessica Siegel spent a summer with a colleague, Bruce Baskind, combing the libraries, community archives and special collections for a new course they planned on the history and literature of the Lower East Side. Their idea was to co-teach a course that would explore the ethnic history of that part of Manhattan from precolonial Indians to contemporary Hispanics and Chinese. The course was a great hit and they became editors as each student produced an oral history of a parent or elder. In June these were collected, typed, duplicated and bound as *Our Lives, Our Stories, Our Neighborhood*.

Escalante found that in addition to discovering how to teach and motivate students of a wide band of abilities, he needed to figure out how to upgrade the curriculum below and to bring teachers in feeder schools into his plan so that more students would have a chance to get into his game. He was successful. There were no calculus classes when he arrived at Garfield. He began with a handful of students in the late 1970s. By 1987 Garfield High School had more students (129) taking calculus AP exams than any other regular public high school in the country. Garfield was then, as when he came, a school serving mostly poor Hispanic youth, with 80 percent of its students qualifying for the federal free- or reduced-lunch program. Nearly 90 percent of its exam-taking students were Hispanic. Only Alhambra High School (177 AP students) in Alhambra, California, where nearly every calculus student came from a middle- or upper-middle-class Asian family, and the two New York City super-schools, where students are admitted by special examination, Stuyvesant (162) and Bronx High School of Science (156), did better. Garfield sent more calculus students to the exam than Exeter or New Trier. The only private school to do better was Andover. Garfield alone accounted for a quarter of the Mexican-American students in the nation who passed the AP calculus exam.

Jessica Siegel had many successes. Her students earned admission to Syracuse and Swarthmore and other colleges. They won journalism awards and special scholarships. Chris Zajac rescued many students, and Mike Rose could take deep satisfaction from seeing many like Olga and Willie achieve success in college.

Why can't we have more such success? Surely we could solve America's educational problems if we had more Siegels and Escalantes leading our classrooms. Yet we aren't even keeping them, let alone attracting replacements. At the age of 38, Jessica Siegel left teaching. Small things, like limited access to a Xerox machine and the lack of any private space to meet with students, and big things like budget cuts and too many long nights reading themes for her 130 students, wore her down. She complained to Freedman that she had no time for a private life and what she wanted were "the normal things, the things that most people already have. I want an easier life. I want a life where I don't just give out without getting anything back." Mike Rose did not stay in public school teaching but moved on to a post in a writing program at UCLA. Readers of *Among Schoolchildren* learn that Chris Zajac suffered the same frustrations as thousands of teachers in inner-city schools. They feel they never have enough time to respond to the real needs of children at the bottom of the social structure. When I called the Kelly School, where Zajac taught fifth grade, I found she had moved to another school to take a position as a language arts specialist that many find less stressful. Jaime Escalante had a heart attack but kept on going. The person who answered the phone at Garfield High said he's still there, though nearing retirement.

My own students, many of them preparing for teaching careers, read these accounts with mixed feelings. They are inspired. But some of them also ask: Are these the kind of sacrifices required to be a good teacher in America? And they are not wrong to ask that question. For we cannot norm a system on saints. We need schools that will attract talented and dedicated people at less than the cost of sainthood, because if we ask that much we are going to be in big trouble filling more than two million teaching positions.

Even if we could find two million saints, they couldn't by themselves compensate for vast inequities that remain in our society — inequities that bring children to school without adequate medical care and send them home to sparse refrigerators in housing projects that have in some cases become huge crack dens. For as good as these teachers were, and as real as their achievements became, from a societal perspective they won small victories. At best the reforms Escalante spurred reached no more than 500 of Garfield High's 3,500 students. At year's end Jessica Siegel found that half of her 134 students had failed, 38 of them due solely to excessive absences. These teachers were evangelists who were trying to give kids a ticket out of poverty, but the poverty remained and blighted many more lives than they could save. When Jessica Siegel left Seward Park, two-fifths of the high schools in New York City operated at more than 110 percent of capacity. Per pupil aid ran nearly 20 percent less than was provided suburban districts. Ninety percent of elementary students had no school library. There was only one counselor for every 600 high school pupils. And now New York is once again threatened with devastating cuts.

Although each of these books is eloquent about the crippling effects of poverty and broken families, evangelists tend to leave such analysis to sociologists. These teachers are like the principal at Seward Park, Noel Kriftcher, who remarks that you can't spend too much time looking at the big picture because it's too depressing. You have to look at one picture at a time.

The causes of failure the teachers address that are most penetrating are closer to home. They lament the frustrations of a mushrooming and frequently insolent bureaucracy. One of many marvelous vignettes in *Small Victories* portrays Siegel's talented colleague Bruce Baskind's attempt to get formally appointed to the school where he has been teaching for several years, long after he obtained all the credentials, passed the required exams and filled out all the forms. Freedman accompanies Bruce for yet one more visit to Board of Education offices at 35 Court Street, where he is shuffled from one office to another and treated as though he were guilty of some stupidity or infraction when he is simply trying to force from the machine a piece of paper — without which he does not have pay or benefits to which he is entitled. In Room 603 a woman behind a desk looks up:

> "'I was checking on the status of my application for employment,' Bruce says humbly.
> 'What are you talking about,' she snaps. 'There's no such thing.'
> Bruce squints, as if he heard wrong. His thick eyebrows press down.
> 'What I mean,' he says, 'is that I gave you those documents over the summer.'
> 'Well, you have to get on the list that you're available.'
> 'But what does that mean,?' Bruce asks. He leans a bit over her desk. Some minor-key irritation creeps into his tone, although any behavior except submission is risky. 'I gave the documents in July. I've been teaching at the school for four years.'
> '*That doesn't matter*,' she says. '*You obviously don't understand.*' She glances at Bruce's face, which is blank in confusion. 'You have to be on the list. We'll call you when we start appointing off the July list.'
> 'When will that be?'
> 'Whenever we do it.'
> She pauses, as if expecting Bruce to excuse himself. A clock ticks. He does not move. 'All right,' she says. 'Room 601.'"

Cutting even closer to the bone, Rose fears that one of the greatest causes of failure lies in the mislabeling teachers do themselves. Once a child is labeled, files thicken and it's almost impossible to reverse early, often unfounded judgments. In teaching 12-year-old Harold, who was slotted into a remedial program, Rose finds the boy begins to respond to what is part teaching and part fathering. (Smaller classes and individual attention are absolutely critical for some children.) He delves into the file and finds that in kindergarten he was tested as "high average" on reading readiness. But his father, who often took him fishing, walked out about that time and was later sent to jail for two years. Harold's teachers began to note he "fidgeted," was easily distracted and had a short attention span. One teacher thought he might need medical help because he was "unpredictable." Another teacher used the more potent word "aphasic," and he was classified "remedial." But soon the remedial teacher felt he was "beyond remediation." None of the medical evaluations, and several were done, ever showed any organic damage. He was a sad and withdrawn boy who began to write beautiful haiku under Rose's watchful care. Rose hoped it was still possible for Harold to overcome the negative labels he had internalized.

These teacher portraits of failure also confirm the analysis of an astute sociologist, Linda McNeil, who has written a dull but exceedingly important book on the *Contradictions of Control*. McNeil's book evolved from a project in which she attempted to find out what teachers actually taught in social studies, especially economics. She suspected that many high school teachers presented a very conservative economic ideology, if they were not guilty of indoctrination. What she found was that most teachers, regardless of their ideology, presented a shamefully oversimplified version of their subjects. And they elicited almost no sense of genuine inquiry. There was little dialogue or questioning or engagement of minds. In the place of an educational exchange they provided lists to be copied and facts to be memorized.

When McNeil interviewed the teachers she found their shortcomings were not because they were poorly educated or did not know how to teach. They said they taught that way because that was what the controllers of the system wanted. Administrators didn't want teachers who rocked the boat or contravened centralized controls. What the system wanted was to move kids through as efficiently as possible. Keep the dropout rate down; turn out graduates with certificates. The system didn't especially want teaching people to think. Teachers wouldn't be rewarded in their paychecks or in any other way for doing the kinds of things Siegel and Escalante and Rose did. As a matter of fact, Escalante himself was passed over for a teaching award in Los Angeles. A union leader who sat on the awards committee had written an article about "sweatshop teachers," arguing that people like Escalante worked students too hard and left them too exhausted to do well in other classes or to enjoy other activities.

McNeil's study shows that there are exceptions — schools where administrators, like the principal at Garfield, value intellectual engagement and work with teachers to put educational goals ahead of control and "efficiency." But in her study of four high schools, all of them superficially regarded as good schools, only one school was so blessed.

McNeil argues that most schools produce "school knowledge," which is an exchange of facts and lists without much real learning or engagement on the part of the students. Although none of the other authors reviewed here was apparently aware of McNeil's work, we find chilling support for her thesis in their reports from the front lines. Mike Rose laments that "what many students experience year after year is the exchange of one body of facts for another — an inert transmission, the delivery and redelivery of segmented and self-contained dates and formulas — and thus it is no surprise that they develop a restricted sense of how intellectual work is conducted." In *Small Victories*, Samuel Freedman captures McNeil's meaning even more eloquently:

> What have these students learned? What have they mastered? The have learned the use of image. They have mastered mirrors. Who has taught them? In part, their teachers. They understand from experience that if you show up (most of the time), hand in homework (every so often), and keep quiet (this is paramount), you will receive your 65 and be permitted to shuffle on toward a diploma and a mortarboard. Appearance is all. . . . "How about the content?" Jessica pled one time. She received only silence in response. It was a foolish question because any student knows that what is important is not comprehending the material; what is important is taking notes so the teacher can see you taking notes; what is important is less being a student than resembling one. The kids call the technique "brain checking."

And this is the great achievement of these teachers. They fought "brain checking," often 14 hours a day, working with many students who had come to believe that maybe they didn't have a brain, or even if they did, what they had to say wouldn't matter anyhow, nobody would pay any attention, would they?

Gerald Grant, the author of *The World We Created at Hamilton High*, is professor of cultural foundations of education at Syracuse University.

Index